BODY MANTRA

SET IN SOUL

THIS JOURNAL BELONGS TO

_____

DEDICATED TO THE NEW BODY THAT IS WAITING FOR ME.

TABLE OF CONTENTS

HOW TO USE THIS JOURNAL

Fitness goals are not easy to stick to for some. You may find that you start then stop. You were doing well for two weeks but then decided to 'treat yourself.' That 'treat yourself' moment ended up overextending itself to now it's your lifestyle and you are back to where you started. Fitness goals require discipline and accountability. You can watch all the fitness videos in the world and write down a ton of fitness goals but if you are not committed to putting in the work required to get the body and health that you want, then you will not see the results you desire.

When it comes to what you should be doing for your body and overall health, it is easy to get swamped with so much information. This fitness journal is here to help you filter out what would work for your body as well as keep track of your results. It is also with this journal that you can really keep yourself accountable. You can keep track of the days that you do and do not work out. You can also create a schedule for yourself and adjust your fitness goals as you need to. By using this journal daily, you will be able to learn if your current routine does or does not work for you as well as find ways to tweak your current workout till you find the ideal fitness lifestyle for you. Remember that because you will be recording your progress, you will be able to see your accumulated efforts over time while looking back on your past journal entries. This builds motivation that will allow you to always give it 100% and keep you focused on your various fitness goals.

We recommend filling out this journal every morning and every night. Under nightly thoughts, if you worked out that day, then fill out the section that applies to that. If you did not work out that day, then fill out that section. Your body is a temple that is important to you. How you want it to look, feel and operate is all on how you treat it. Use this journal to set your plan and to create your body mantra. Watch your body conform to the vision you have for it as you put in the work. We know you can do it. Let's get started.

FITNESS GOALS

MY PAST FITNESS GOALS

MY CURRENT FITNESS GOALS

MY BODILY INJURIES

MY BODILY INJURIES

(List Past And Current Body Injuries)

MY DIET

MY OLD DIET

MY NEW DIET

MY FITNESS PLAN

MY NEW FITNESS PLAN

THE
REPROGRAMMING

THE REPROGRAMMING

I Currently Weight:

I Want To Work On:

I Currently View Myself:

I Started Noticing:

I Want To Gain Control Over:

THE REPROGRAMMING

I Feel Good When I:

I Do Not Feel Good When I:

I Want To Get Fit Because:

Am I An Energetic Person?

What Are My Short Term Fitness Goals?

THE REPROGRAMMING

What Are My Long Term Fitness Goals?

Someone I Admire Who I Believe Is Fit:

What Do I Want To Be Able To Do?

Am I A Dedicated Person?

If I Responded No To The Previous Prompt, How Can I Become Dedicated?

THE REPROGRAMMING

Am I A Consistent Person?

If I Responded No To The Previous Prompt, How Can I Become More Consistent?

Do I Make Excuses?

Am I Working With A Trainer?

Will I Be Working With A Trainer?

THE REPROGRAMMING

If I Responded Yes To The Two Previous Prompts, Then Who Is/Will Be My Trainer And What Makes Them Qualified To Train Me?

Does My Current Diet Align With My Ideal Body?

Is My Current Fitness Goals Realistic For Me?

How Dedicated Am I To Creating My New Fitness Lifestyle?

What Motivates Me To Get Fit?

THE REPROGRAMMING

What Is Challenging To Me?

What Is My New Mindset?

What Was My Old Mindset?

Do I Currently Workout?

If I Responded Yes To The Previous Prompt, What Would Make My Current Workouts Better?

THE REPROGRAMMING

How Can I Make My Workouts Fun?

Do I Have Visual Goals?

If I Responded Yes To The Previous Prompt, What Are They?

If I Responded No To The Second Prompt On This Page, Why Not?

Do I Have A Workout Buddy?

THE REPROGRAMMING

If I Responded Yes To The Previous Prompt, Who Is My Workout Buddy?

What Is My Current Exercise Playlist?

What Is Considered 'Too Much' When Exercising?

What Does My New Fitness Lifestyle Looklike?

What Habits Do I Currently Have That Go Against My Ideal Fitness Lifestyle?

THE REPROGRAMMING

What Are My Current Strengths?

What Are My Current Weaknesses?

I Want To Have The Strength To:

Do I Currently Have A Membership At A Gym?

If I Responded Yes To The Previous Prompt, With What Gym Do I Currently Have A Gym Membership And Do I Currently Use My Gym Membership?

THE REPROGRAMMING

Do I Believe I Need A Gym Membership To Reach My Fitness Goals?

What Kinds Of Research Have I Done Towards Certain Exercises In Connection With My Body Type?

What Exercises Work Well For My Body Type?

What Is The Most Effective Calorie-Burning Workout For Me?

What Kinds Of Exercises Will I Engage In?

THE REPROGRAMMING

What Days Of The Week Will I Be Exercising?

What Times Of The Day Will I Be Exercising?

How Long Will I Work Out For?

What Days Do I Plan To Rest?

How Will I Make It A Priority To Workout?

THE REPROGRAMMING

Am I Emotionally Prepared For My Fitness Journey?

If I Responded No To The Previous Prompt, How Can I Become Emotionally Prepared For My Fitness Journey?

What Can I Expect During My Fitness Journey?

Do I Have The Right Fitness Gear?

If I Responded No To The Previous Prompt, Do I Need The Right Fitness Gear?

THE REPROGRAMMING

Who Supports My Fitness Journey?

I View Soreness As:

Each Night I Go To Sleep At:

How Many Hours Of Sleep Do I Typically Get?

Typically Breakfast Consists Of:

THE REPROGRAMMING

Typically Lunch Consists Of:

Typically Dinner Consists Of:

I Normally Snack On:

What Supplements Do I Currently Take Or Plan To Take?

How Do I Practice Mindfulness?

THE REPROGRAMMING

I Want To Change:

Past Health Goals I Never Followed Through With:

What Have I Been Putting Off?

What Is My Current Morning Ritual?

What Is My Biggest Barrier?

THE REPROGRAMMING

I Am Not Sure About:

I Need Instructions On:

I Want To Start/Continue Exercising Now Because:

What Is Bothering Me?

Am I Currently Active?

THE REPROGRAMMING

What Exercises Do I Like?

What Exercises Do I Dislike?

What Exercises Make Me Feel Good?

My New Fitness Routine Will Be:

What Kinds Of Results Do I Want To See?

THE REPROGRAMMING

With The Results, How Do I Want To Feel?

I Know I Can Transform My Body To:

I Want My Body To Look:

Have I Quit My Fitness Goals Before?

If I Responded Yes To The Previous Prompt, Why Did I Quit My Previous Fitness Goals And What Will Make It Different This Time?

THE REPROGRAMMING

What Would Get Me To Quit My Fitness Goals?

What Do I Want To See Change Within Me As Well As Outside Of Me?

Will I Be Doing Any Indoor Exercises?

I Believe:

I Want My Body To Feel:

THE REPROGRAMMING

I Will Not:

A Promise I Am Making To Myself:

What Would I Look At Daily To Keep Me Going?

I Know It Will Take Time To:

Throwing Up Is:

THE REPROGRAMMING

Sweat Is:

What Exercises Do I Struggle With Now That I Will Like The Ability To Do With Ease Soon?

Will I Be Taking Any Fitness Classes?

If I Responded Yes To The Previous Prompt, Which Ones?

When Will I Start My Fitness Journey?

THE REPROGRAMMING

I Will Be Focusing On:

What Will It Take For Me To Lose Weight?

What Will It Take For Me To Gain Weight?

When I See Other People Who Are At My Fitness Goal:

When I See Other People Working Out:

THE REPROGRAMMING

I Had To Cut Out:

I Have To Increase:

Am I Self-Conscience About How I Look While Working Out?

How Long Am I Giving Myself To Reach My Goals?

I Will Not Worry About:

THE REPROGRAMMING

I Will Stay Present By:

I Will Allow:

What Will I Not Allow To Distract Me And/Or Discourage Me?

Everyday Is A Great Day To:

I Know I Can:

THE REPROGRAMMING

I Choose To Now Live:

Fitness Is Important Because:

Even When My Body Is Sore:

I Want To Gain More:

I Am Currently Able To Lift:

THE REPROGRAMMING

Am I Flexible?

Strength Training Is:

Aerobic Exercises Will Help Me:

How Will My Exercises Vary?

MY NEW BODY

NEW BODY THIS MORNING

Date: Mood:

Today's Declaration:

My Body Is:

My Body Feels:

I Thank God For:

Today I Will Focus On:

My Exercise Goal For Today:

Today's Self-Talk:

MY NEW BODY - NIGHTLY THOUGHTS

Date:

IF I DID NOT WORK OUT TODAY
(FILL OUT THE FOLLOWING)....

How Did I Relax My Body Today?

What Changes Am I Starting To Notice?

Today I Allowed Myself:

Who Tried To Discourage Me From Working Out Today?

IF I WORKED OUT TODAY
(FILL OUT THE FOLLOWING)....

Work Out Time:

Length Of Time Spent Working Out:

My Exercise Heart Rate:

My Heart Rate Resting:

I Motivated Myself By:

My Workout Today Consisted Of:

Equipment That I Used Today:

While Working Out Today, I Listened To:

Did I Have A Workout Partner/Trainer Today And If The Answer Is Yes, Who Was It?

Today I Ate:

Today I Drank:

NIGHTLY THOUGHTS CONTINUED

Classes I Took Today (Answer If Applicable):

I Noticed:

What Parts Of My Body Feel Sore Today?

I No Longer Complain About:

What Felt Good Today?

What Tried To Discourage Me Today From Working Out?

What Did Not Feel Good Today?

I Took Advantage Of:

What Was A Challenge For Me Today?

I Am Progressing Towards:

I Am Working Through:

NEW BODY THIS MORNING

Date:

Mood:

Today's Declaration:

My Body Is:

My Body Feels:

I Thank God For:

Today I Will Focus On:

My Exercise Goal For Today:

Today's Self-Talk:

MY NEW BODY - NIGHTLY THOUGHTS

Date:

IF I DID NOT WORK OUT TODAY
(FILL OUT THE FOLLOWING)....

How Did I Relax My Body Today?

Today I Allowed Myself:

What Changes Am I Starting To Notice?

Who Tried To Discourage Me From
Working Out Today?

IF I WORKED OUT TODAY
(FILL OUT THE FOLLOWING)....

Work Out Time:

Equipment That I Used Today:

Length Of Time Spent Working Out:

While Working Out Today, I Listened To:

My Exercise Heart Rate:

Did I Have A Workout Partner/Trainer Today
And If The Answer Is Yes, Who Was It?

My Heart Rate Resting:

I Motivated Myself By:

Today I Ate:

My Workout Today Consisted Of:

Today I Drank:

NIGHTLY THOUGHTS CONTINUED

Classes I Took Today (Answer If Applicable):

I Noticed:

What Parts Of My Body Feel Sore Today?

I No Longer Complain About:

What Felt Good Today?

What Tried To Discourage Me Today From Working Out?

What Did Not Feel Good Today?

I Took Advantage Of:

What Was A Challenge For Me Today?

I Am Progressing Towards:

I Am Working Through:

NO EXCUSES.

MY BODY WILL THANK ME.

NEW BODY THIS MORNING

Date: Mood:

Today's Declaration:

My Body Is:

My Body Feels:

I Thank God For:

Today I Will Focus On:

My Exercise Goal For Today:

Today's Self-Talk:

MY NEW BODY - NIGHTLY THOUGHTS

Date:

IF I DID NOT WORK OUT TODAY
(FILL OUT THE FOLLOWING)....

How Did I Relax My Body Today?

Today I Allowed Myself:

What Changes Am I Starting To Notice?

Who Tried To Discourage Me From Working Out Today?

IF I WORKED OUT TODAY
(FILL OUT THE FOLLOWING)....

Work Out Time:

Equipment That I Used Today:

Length Of Time Spent Working Out:

While Working Out Today, I Listened To:

My Exercise Heart Rate:

Did I Have A Workout Partner/Trainer Today And If The Answer Is Yes, Who Was It?

My Heart Rate Resting:

I Motivated Myself By:

Today I Ate:

My Workout Today Consisted Of:

Today I Drank:

NIGHTLY THOUGHTS CONTINUED

Classes I Took Today (Answer If Applicable):

I Noticed:

What Parts Of My Body Feel Sore Today?

I No Longer Complain About:

What Felt Good Today?

What Tried To Discourage Me Today From Working Out?

What Did Not Feel Good Today?

I Took Advantage Of:

What Was A Challenge For Me Today?

I Am Progressing Towards:

I Am Working Through:

NEW BODY THIS MORNING

Date: Mood:

Today's Declaration:

My Body Is:

My Body Feels:

I Thank God For:

Today I Will Focus On:

My Exercise Goal For Today:

Today's Self-Talk:

MY NEW BODY - NIGHTLY THOUGHTS

Date:

IF I DID NOT WORK OUT TODAY
(FILL OUT THE FOLLOWING)....

How Did I Relax My Body Today?

Today I Allowed Myself:

What Changes Am I Starting To Notice?

Who Tried To Discourage Me From
Working Out Today?

IF I WORKED OUT TODAY
(FILL OUT THE FOLLOWING)....

Work Out Time:

Equipment That I Used Today:

Length Of Time Spent Working Out:

While Working Out Today, I Listened To:

My Exercise Heart Rate:

Did I Have A Workout Partner/Trainer Today
And If The Answer Is Yes, Who Was It?

My Heart Rate Resting:

I Motivated Myself By:

Today I Ate:

My Workout Today Consisted Of:

Today I Drank:

NIGHTLY THOUGHTS CONTINUED

Classes I Took Today (Answer If Applicable):

I Noticed:

What Parts Of My Body Feel Sore Today?

I No Longer Complain About:

What Felt Good Today?

What Tried To Discourage Me Today From Working Out?

What Did Not Feel Good Today?

I Took Advantage Of:

What Was A Challenge For Me Today?

I Am Progressing Towards:

I Am Working Through:

NEW BODY THIS MORNING

Date: Mood:

Today's Declaration:

My Body Is:

My Body Feels:

I Thank God For:

Today I Will Focus On:

My Exercise Goal For Today:

Today's Self-Talk:

MY NEW BODY - NIGHTLY THOUGHTS

Date:

IF I DID NOT WORK OUT TODAY
(FILL OUT THE FOLLOWING)....

How Did I Relax My Body Today?

What Changes Am I Starting To Notice?

Today I Allowed Myself:

Who Tried To Discourage Me From Working Out Today?

IF I WORKED OUT TODAY
(FILL OUT THE FOLLOWING)....

Work Out Time:

Length Of Time Spent Working Out:

My Exercise Heart Rate:

My Heart Rate Resting:

I Motivated Myself By:

My Workout Today Consisted Of:

Equipment That I Used Today:

While Working Out Today, I Listened To:

Did I Have A Workout Partner/Trainer Today And If The Answer Is Yes, Who Was It?

Today I Ate:

Today I Drank:

NIGHTLY THOUGHTS CONTINUED

Classes I Took Today (Answer If Applicable):

I Noticed:

What Parts Of My Body Feel Sore Today?

I No Longer Complain About:

What Felt Good Today?

What Tried To Discourage Me Today From Working Out?

What Did Not Feel Good Today?

I Took Advantage Of:

What Was A Challenge For Me Today?

I Am Progressing Towards:

I Am Working Through:

TODAY I FELT PAIN AND I OVERCAME IT.

PERSONAL THOUGHTS

NEW BODY THIS MORNING

Date: Mood:

Today's Declaration:

My Body Is:

My Body Feels:

I Thank God For:

Today I Will Focus On:

My Exercise Goal For Today:

Today's Self-Talk:

MY NEW BODY - NIGHTLY THOUGHTS

Date:

IF I DID NOT WORK OUT TODAY
(FILL OUT THE FOLLOWING)....

How Did I Relax My Body Today?

Today I Allowed Myself:

What Changes Am I Starting To Notice?

Who Tried To Discourage Me From
Working Out Today?

IF I WORKED OUT TODAY
(FILL OUT THE FOLLOWING)....

Work Out Time:

Equipment That I Used Today:

Length Of Time Spent Working Out:

While Working Out Today, I Listened To:

My Exercise Heart Rate:

Did I Have A Workout Partner/Trainer Today
And If The Answer Is Yes, Who Was It?

My Heart Rate Resting:

I Motivated Myself By:

Today I Ate:

My Workout Today Consisted Of:

Today I Drank:

NIGHTLY THOUGHTS CONTINUED

Classes I Took Today (Answer If Applicable):

I Noticed:

What Parts Of My Body Feel Sore Today?

I No Longer Complain About:

What Felt Good Today?

What Tried To Discourage Me Today From Working Out?

What Did Not Feel Good Today?

I Took Advantage Of:

What Was A Challenge For Me Today?

I Am Progressing Towards:

I Am Working Through:

NEW BODY THIS MORNING

Date: Mood:

Today's Declaration:

My Body Is:

My Body Feels:

I Thank God For:

Today I Will Focus On:

My Exercise Goal For Today:

Today's Self-Talk:

MY NEW BODY - NIGHTLY THOUGHTS

Date:

IF I DID NOT WORK OUT TODAY
(FILL OUT THE FOLLOWING)....

How Did I Relax My Body Today?

Today I Allowed Myself:

What Changes Am I Starting To Notice?

Who Tried To Discourage Me From Working Out Today?

IF I WORKED OUT TODAY
(FILL OUT THE FOLLOWING)....

Work Out Time:

Equipment That I Used Today:

Length Of Time Spent Working Out:

While Working Out Today, I Listened To:

My Exercise Heart Rate:

Did I Have A Workout Partner/Trainer Today And If The Answer Is Yes, Who Was It?

My Heart Rate Resting:

I Motivated Myself By:

Today I Ate:

My Workout Today Consisted Of:

Today I Drank:

NIGHTLY THOUGHTS CONTINUED

Classes I Took Today (Answer If Applicable):

I Noticed:

What Parts Of My Body Feel Sore Today?

I No Longer Complain About:

What Felt Good Today?

What Tried To Discourage Me Today From Working Out?

What Did Not Feel Good Today?

I Took Advantage Of:

What Was A Challenge For Me Today?

I Am Progressing Towards:

I Am Working Through:

#PERSEVERANCE

IT IS THE MENTAL THAT CHANGES MY PHYSICAL.

NEW BODY THIS MORNING

Date: Mood:

Today's Declaration:

My Body Is:

My Body Feels:

I Thank God For:

Today I Will Focus On:

My Exercise Goal For Today:

Today's Self-Talk:

MY NEW BODY - NIGHTLY THOUGHTS

Date:

IF I DID NOT WORK OUT TODAY
(FILL OUT THE FOLLOWING)....

How Did I Relax My Body Today?

Today I Allowed Myself:

What Changes Am I Starting To Notice?

Who Tried To Discourage Me From Working Out Today?

IF I WORKED OUT TODAY
(FILL OUT THE FOLLOWING)....

Work Out Time:

Equipment That I Used Today:

Length Of Time Spent Working Out:

While Working Out Today, I Listened To:

My Exercise Heart Rate:

Did I Have A Workout Partner/Trainer Today And If The Answer Is Yes, Who Was It?

My Heart Rate Resting:

I Motivated Myself By:

Today I Ate:

My Workout Today Consisted Of:

Today I Drank:

NIGHTLY THOUGHTS CONTINUED

Classes I Took Today (Answer If Applicable):

I Noticed:

What Parts Of My Body Feel Sore Today?

I No Longer Complain About:

What Felt Good Today?

What Tried To Discourage Me Today From Working Out?

What Did Not Feel Good Today?

I Took Advantage Of:

What Was A Challenge For Me Today?

I Am Progressing Towards:

I Am Working Through:

NEW BODY THIS MORNING

Date: Mood:

Today's Declaration:

My Body Is:

My Body Feels:

I Thank God For:

Today I Will Focus On:

My Exercise Goal For Today:

Today's Self-Talk:

MY NEW BODY - NIGHTLY THOUGHTS

Date:

IF I DID NOT WORK OUT TODAY
(FILL OUT THE FOLLOWING)....

How Did I Relax My Body Today?

Today I Allowed Myself:

What Changes Am I Starting To Notice?

Who Tried To Discourage Me From Working Out Today?

IF I WORKED OUT TODAY
(FILL OUT THE FOLLOWING)....

Work Out Time:

Equipment That I Used Today:

Length Of Time Spent Working Out:

While Working Out Today, I Listened To:

My Exercise Heart Rate:

Did I Have A Workout Partner/Trainer Today And If The Answer Is Yes, Who Was It?

My Heart Rate Resting:

I Motivated Myself By:

Today I Ate:

My Workout Today Consisted Of:

Today I Drank:

NIGHTLY THOUGHTS CONTINUED

Classes I Took Today (Answer If Applicable):

I Noticed:

What Parts Of My Body Feel Sore Today?

I No Longer Complain About:

What Felt Good Today?

What Tried To Discourage Me Today From Working Out?

What Did Not Feel Good Today?

I Took Advantage Of:

What Was A Challenge For Me Today?

I Am Progressing Towards:

I Am Working Through:

MY IDEAL BODY IS....

I WORKED FOR EVERY SINGLE MUSCLE.

NEW BODY THIS MORNING

Date: Mood:

Today's Declaration:

My Body Is:

My Body Feels:

I Thank God For:

Today I Will Focus On:

My Exercise Goal For Today:

Today's Self-Talk:

MY NEW BODY - NIGHTLY THOUGHTS

Date:

IF I DID NOT WORK OUT TODAY
(FILL OUT THE FOLLOWING)....

How Did I Relax My Body Today?

Today I Allowed Myself:

What Changes Am I Starting To Notice?

Who Tried To Discourage Me From Working Out Today?

IF I WORKED OUT TODAY
(FILL OUT THE FOLLOWING)....

Work Out Time:

Equipment That I Used Today:

Length Of Time Spent Working Out:

While Working Out Today, I Listened To:

My Exercise Heart Rate:

Did I Have A Workout Partner/Trainer Today And If The Answer Is Yes, Who Was It?

My Heart Rate Resting:

I Motivated Myself By:

Today I Ate:

My Workout Today Consisted Of:

Today I Drank:

NIGHTLY THOUGHTS CONTINUED

Classes I Took Today (Answer If Applicable):

I Noticed:

What Parts Of My Body Feel Sore Today?

I No Longer Complain About:

What Felt Good Today?

What Tried To Discourage Me Today From Working Out?

What Did Not Feel Good Today?

I Took Advantage Of:

What Was A Challenge For Me Today?

I Am Progressing Towards:

I Am Working Through:

NEW BODY THIS MORNING

Date: Mood:

Today's Declaration:

My Body Is:

My Body Feels:

I Thank God For:

Today I Will Focus On:

My Exercise Goal For Today:

Today's Self-Talk:

MY NEW BODY - NIGHTLY THOUGHTS

Date:

IF I DID NOT WORK OUT TODAY
(FILL OUT THE FOLLOWING)....

How Did I Relax My Body Today?

Today I Allowed Myself:

What Changes Am I Starting To Notice?

Who Tried To Discourage Me From
Working Out Today?

IF I WORKED OUT TODAY
(FILL OUT THE FOLLOWING)....

Work Out Time:

Equipment That I Used Today:

Length Of Time Spent Working Out:

While Working Out Today, I Listened To:

My Exercise Heart Rate:

Did I Have A Workout Partner/Trainer Today
And If The Answer Is Yes, Who Was It?

My Heart Rate Resting:

I Motivated Myself By:

Today I Ate:

My Workout Today Consisted Of:

Today I Drank:

NIGHTLY THOUGHTS CONTINUED

Classes I Took Today (Answer If Applicable):

I Noticed:

What Parts Of My Body Feel Sore Today?

I No Longer Complain About:

What Felt Good Today?

What Tried To Discourage Me Today From Working Out?

What Did Not Feel Good Today?

I Took Advantage Of:

What Was A Challenge For Me Today?

I Am Progressing Towards:

I Am Working Through:

I AM TURNING INTO THE BEST VERSION OF MYSELF.

PERSONAL THOUGHTS

NEW BODY THIS MORNING

Date: Mood:

Today's Declaration:

My Body Is:

My Body Feels:

I Thank God For:

Today I Will Focus On:

My Exercise Goal For Today:

Today's Self-Talk:

MY NEW BODY - NIGHTLY THOUGHTS

Date:

IF I DID NOT WORK OUT TODAY
(FILL OUT THE FOLLOWING)....

How Did I Relax My Body Today?

Today I Allowed Myself:

What Changes Am I Starting To Notice?

Who Tried To Discourage Me From Working Out Today?

IF I WORKED OUT TODAY
(FILL OUT THE FOLLOWING)....

Work Out Time:

Equipment That I Used Today:

Length Of Time Spent Working Out:

While Working Out Today, I Listened To:

My Exercise Heart Rate:

Did I Have A Workout Partner/Trainer Today And If The Answer Is Yes, Who Was It?

My Heart Rate Resting:

I Motivated Myself By:

Today I Ate:

My Workout Today Consisted Of:

Today I Drank:

NIGHTLY THOUGHTS CONTINUED

Classes I Took Today (Answer If Applicable):

I Noticed:

What Parts Of My Body Feel Sore Today?

I No Longer Complain About:

What Felt Good Today?

What Tried To Discourage Me Today From Working Out?

What Did Not Feel Good Today?

I Took Advantage Of:

What Was A Challenge For Me Today?

I Am Progressing Towards:

I Am Working Through:

NEW BODY THIS MORNING

Date: Mood:

Today's Declaration:

My Body Is:

My Body Feels:

I Thank God For:

Today I Will Focus On:

My Exercise Goal For Today:

Today's Self-Talk:

MY NEW BODY - NIGHTLY THOUGHTS

Date:

IF I DID NOT WORK OUT TODAY
(FILL OUT THE FOLLOWING)....

How Did I Relax My Body Today?

What Changes Am I Starting To Notice?

Today I Allowed Myself:

Who Tried To Discourage Me From Working Out Today?

IF I WORKED OUT TODAY
(FILL OUT THE FOLLOWING)....

Work Out Time:

Length Of Time Spent Working Out:

My Exercise Heart Rate:

My Heart Rate Resting:

I Motivated Myself By:

My Workout Today Consisted Of:

Equipment That I Used Today:

While Working Out Today, I Listened To:

Did I Have A Workout Partner/Trainer Today And If The Answer Is Yes, Who Was It?

Today I Ate:

Today I Drank:

NIGHTLY THOUGHTS CONTINUED

Classes I Took Today (Answer If Applicable):

I Noticed:

What Parts Of My Body Feel Sore Today?

I No Longer Complain About:

What Felt Good Today?

What Tried To Discourage Me Today From Working Out?

What Did Not Feel Good Today?

I Took Advantage Of:

What Was A Challenge For Me Today?

I Am Progressing Towards:

I Am Working Through:

A BODY IN MOVEMENT PRODUCES POSITIVE ENERGY.

THIS IS A LIFESTYLE.

NEW BODY THIS MORNING

Date: Mood:

Today's Declaration:

My Body Is:

My Body Feels:

I Thank God For:

Today I Will Focus On:

My Exercise Goal For Today:

Today's Self-Talk:

MY NEW BODY - NIGHTLY THOUGHTS

Date:

IF I DID NOT WORK OUT TODAY
(FILL OUT THE FOLLOWING)....

How Did I Relax My Body Today?

Today I Allowed Myself:

What Changes Am I Starting To Notice?

Who Tried To Discourage Me From
Working Out Today?

IF I WORKED OUT TODAY
(FILL OUT THE FOLLOWING)....

Work Out Time:

Equipment That I Used Today:

Length Of Time Spent Working Out:

While Working Out Today, I Listened To:

My Exercise Heart Rate:

Did I Have A Workout Partner/Trainer Today
And If The Answer Is Yes, Who Was It?

My Heart Rate Resting:

I Motivated Myself By:

Today I Ate:

My Workout Today Consisted Of:

Today I Drank:

NIGHTLY THOUGHTS CONTINUED

Classes I Took Today (Answer If Applicable):

I Noticed:

What Parts Of My Body Feel Sore Today?

I No Longer Complain About:

What Felt Good Today?

What Tried To Discourage Me Today From Working Out?

What Did Not Feel Good Today?

I Took Advantage Of:

What Was A Challenge For Me Today?

I Am Progressing Towards:

I Am Working Through:

NEW BODY THIS MORNING

Date: Mood:

Today's Declaration:

My Body Is:

My Body Feels:

I Thank God For:

Today I Will Focus On:

My Exercise Goal For Today:

Today's Self-Talk:

MY NEW BODY - NIGHTLY THOUGHTS

Date:

IF I DID NOT WORK OUT TODAY
(FILL OUT THE FOLLOWING)....

How Did I Relax My Body Today?

Today I Allowed Myself:

What Changes Am I Starting To Notice?

Who Tried To Discourage Me From Working Out Today?

IF I WORKED OUT TODAY
(FILL OUT THE FOLLOWING)....

Work Out Time:

Equipment That I Used Today:

Length Of Time Spent Working Out:

While Working Out Today, I Listened To:

My Exercise Heart Rate:

Did I Have A Workout Partner/Trainer Today And If The Answer Is Yes, Who Was It?

My Heart Rate Resting:

I Motivated Myself By:

Today I Ate:

My Workout Today Consisted Of:

Today I Drank:

NIGHTLY THOUGHTS CONTINUED

Classes I Took Today (Answer If Applicable):

I Noticed:

What Parts Of My Body Feel Sore Today?

I No Longer Complain About:

What Felt Good Today?

What Tried To Discourage Me Today From Working Out?

What Did Not Feel Good Today?

I Took Advantage Of:

What Was A Challenge For Me Today?

I Am Progressing Towards:

I Am Working Through:

EXERCISING THE MIND AND BODY.

WHO HAS INFLUENCED ME?

NEW BODY THIS MORNING

Date: Mood:

Today's Declaration:

My Body Is:

My Body Feels:

I Thank God For:

Today I Will Focus On:

My Exercise Goal For Today:

Today's Self-Talk:

MY NEW BODY - NIGHTLY THOUGHTS

Date:

IF I DID NOT WORK OUT TODAY
(FILL OUT THE FOLLOWING)....

How Did I Relax My Body Today?

Today I Allowed Myself:

What Changes Am I Starting To Notice?

Who Tried To Discourage Me From Working Out Today?

IF I WORKED OUT TODAY
(FILL OUT THE FOLLOWING)....

Work Out Time:

Equipment That I Used Today:

Length Of Time Spent Working Out:

While Working Out Today, I Listened To:

My Exercise Heart Rate:

Did I Have A Workout Partner/Trainer Today And If The Answer Is Yes, Who Was It?

My Heart Rate Resting:

I Motivated Myself By:

Today I Ate:

My Workout Today Consisted Of:

Today I Drank:

NIGHTLY THOUGHTS CONTINUED

Classes I Took Today (Answer If Applicable):

What Parts Of My Body Feel Sore Today?

What Felt Good Today?

What Did Not Feel Good Today?

What Was A Challenge For Me Today?

I Am Working Through:

I Noticed:

I No Longer Complain About:

What Tried To Discourage Me Today From Working Out?

I Took Advantage Of:

I Am Progressing Towards:

NEW BODY THIS MORNING

Date: Mood:

Today's Declaration:

My Body Is:

My Body Feels:

I Thank God For:

Today I Will Focus On:

My Exercise Goal For Today:

Today's Self-Talk:

MY NEW BODY – NIGHTLY THOUGHTS

Date:

IF I DID NOT WORK OUT TODAY
(FILL OUT THE FOLLOWING)....

How Did I Relax My Body Today?

Today I Allowed Myself:

What Changes Am I Starting To Notice?

Who Tried To Discourage Me From Working Out Today?

IF I WORKED OUT TODAY
(FILL OUT THE FOLLOWING)....

Work Out Time:

Equipment That I Used Today:

Length Of Time Spent Working Out:

While Working Out Today, I Listened To:

My Exercise Heart Rate:

Did I Have A Workout Partner/Trainer Today And If The Answer Is Yes, Who Was It?

My Heart Rate Resting:

I Motivated Myself By:

Today I Ate:

My Workout Today Consisted Of:

Today I Drank:

NIGHTLY THOUGHTS CONTINUED

Classes I Took Today (Answer If Applicable):

I Noticed:

What Parts Of My Body Feel Sore Today?

I No Longer Complain About:

What Felt Good Today?

What Tried To Discourage Me Today From Working Out?

What Did Not Feel Good Today?

I Took Advantage Of:

What Was A Challenge For Me Today?

I Am Progressing Towards:

I Am Working Through:

NEW BODY THIS MORNING

Date: Mood:

Today's Declaration:

My Body Is:

My Body Feels:

I Thank God For:

Today I Will Focus On:

My Exercise Goal For Today:

Today's Self-Talk:

MY NEW BODY - NIGHTLY THOUGHTS

Date:

IF I DID NOT WORK OUT TODAY
(FILL OUT THE FOLLOWING)....

How Did I Relax My Body Today?

Today I Allowed Myself:

What Changes Am I Starting To Notice?

Who Tried To Discourage Me From
Working Out Today?

IF I WORKED OUT TODAY
(FILL OUT THE FOLLOWING)....

Work Out Time:

Equipment That I Used Today:

Length Of Time Spent Working Out:

While Working Out Today, I Listened To:

My Exercise Heart Rate:

Did I Have A Workout Partner/Trainer Today
And If The Answer Is Yes, Who Was It?

My Heart Rate Resting:

I Motivated Myself By:

Today I Ate:

My Workout Today Consisted Of:

Today I Drank:

NIGHTLY THOUGHTS CONTINUED

Classes I Took Today (Answer If Applicable):

I Noticed:

What Parts Of My Body Feel Sore Today?

I No Longer Complain About:

What Felt Good Today?

What Tried To Discourage Me Today From Working Out?

What Did Not Feel Good Today?

I Took Advantage Of:

What Was A Challenge For Me Today?

I Am Progressing Towards:

I Am Working Through:

PERSONAL THOUGHTS

THINGS ARE IMPROVING FOR ME.

NEW BODY THIS MORNING

Date: Mood:

Today's Declaration:

My Body Is:

My Body Feels:

I Thank God For:

Today I Will Focus On:

My Exercise Goal For Today:

Today's Self-Talk:

MY NEW BODY - NIGHTLY THOUGHTS

Date:

IF I DID NOT WORK OUT TODAY
(FILL OUT THE FOLLOWING)....

How Did I Relax My Body Today?

What Changes Am I Starting To Notice?

Today I Allowed Myself:

Who Tried To Discourage Me From Working Out Today?

IF I WORKED OUT TODAY
(FILL OUT THE FOLLOWING)....

Work Out Time:

Length Of Time Spent Working Out:

My Exercise Heart Rate:

My Heart Rate Resting:

I Motivated Myself By:

My Workout Today Consisted Of:

Equipment That I Used Today:

While Working Out Today, I Listened To:

Did I Have A Workout Partner/Trainer Today And If The Answer Is Yes, Who Was It?

Today I Ate:

Today I Drank:

NIGHTLY THOUGHTS CONTINUED

Classes I Took Today (Answer If Applicable):

I Noticed:

What Parts Of My Body Feel Sore Today?

I No Longer Complain About:

What Felt Good Today?

What Tried To Discourage Me Today From Working Out?

What Did Not Feel Good Today?

I Took Advantage Of:

What Was A Challenge For Me Today?

I Am Progressing Towards:

I Am Working Through:

NEW BODY THIS MORNING

Date: Mood:

Today's Declaration:

My Body Is:

My Body Feels:

I Thank God For:

Today I Will Focus On:

My Exercise Goal For Today:

Today's Self-Talk:

MY NEW BODY - NIGHTLY THOUGHTS

Date:

IF I DID NOT WORK OUT TODAY
(FILL OUT THE FOLLOWING)....

How Did I Relax My Body Today?

Today I Allowed Myself:

What Changes Am I Starting To Notice?

Who Tried To Discourage Me From
Working Out Today?

IF I WORKED OUT TODAY
(FILL OUT THE FOLLOWING)....

Work Out Time:

Equipment That I Used Today:

Length Of Time Spent Working Out:

While Working Out Today, I Listened To:

My Exercise Heart Rate:

Did I Have A Workout Partner/Trainer Today
And If The Answer Is Yes, Who Was It?

My Heart Rate Resting:

I Motivated Myself By:

Today I Ate:

My Workout Today Consisted Of:

Today I Drank:

NIGHTLY THOUGHTS CONTINUED

Classes I Took Today (Answer If Applicable):

I Noticed:

What Parts Of My Body Feel Sore Today?

I No Longer Complain About:

What Felt Good Today?

What Tried To Discourage Me Today From Working Out?

What Did Not Feel Good Today?

I Took Advantage Of:

What Was A Challenge For Me Today?

I Am Progressing Towards:

I Am Working Through:

NEW BODY THIS MORNING

Date: Mood:

Today's Declaration:

My Body Is:

My Body Feels:

I Thank God For:

Today I Will Focus On:

My Exercise Goal For Today:

Today's Self-Talk:

MY NEW BODY - NIGHTLY THOUGHTS

Date:

IF I DID NOT WORK OUT TODAY
(FILL OUT THE FOLLOWING)....

How Did I Relax My Body Today?

Today I Allowed Myself:

What Changes Am I Starting To Notice?

Who Tried To Discourage Me From
Working Out Today?

IF I WORKED OUT TODAY
(FILL OUT THE FOLLOWING)....

Work Out Time:

Equipment That I Used Today:

Length Of Time Spent Working Out:

While Working Out Today, I Listened To:

My Exercise Heart Rate:

Did I Have A Workout Partner/Trainer Today
And If The Answer Is Yes, Who Was It?

My Heart Rate Resting:

I Motivated Myself By:

Today I Ate:

My Workout Today Consisted Of:

Today I Drank:

NIGHTLY THOUGHTS CONTINUED

Classes I Took Today (Answer If Applicable):

I Noticed:

What Parts Of My Body Feel Sore Today?

I No Longer Complain About:

What Felt Good Today?

What Tried To Discourage Me Today From Working Out?

What Did Not Feel Good Today?

I Took Advantage Of:

What Was A Challenge For Me Today?

I Am Progressing Towards:

I Am Working Through:

THIS IS NOT AN OVERNIGHT PROCESS. THIS IS AN OVER TIME PROCESS.

TO ME, BEING HEALTHY MEANS....

NEW BODY THIS MORNING

Date: Mood:

Today's Declaration:

My Body Is:

My Body Feels:

I Thank God For:

Today I Will Focus On:

My Exercise Goal For Today:

Today's Self-Talk:

MY NEW BODY - NIGHTLY THOUGHTS

Date:

IF I DID NOT WORK OUT TODAY
(FILL OUT THE FOLLOWING)....

How Did I Relax My Body Today?

Today I Allowed Myself:

What Changes Am I Starting To Notice?

Who Tried To Discourage Me From
Working Out Today?

IF I WORKED OUT TODAY
(FILL OUT THE FOLLOWING)....

Work Out Time:

Equipment That I Used Today:

Length Of Time Spent Working Out:

While Working Out Today, I Listened To:

My Exercise Heart Rate:

Did I Have A Workout Partner/Trainer Today
And If The Answer Is Yes, Who Was It?

My Heart Rate Resting:

I Motivated Myself By:

Today I Ate:

My Workout Today Consisted Of:

Today I Drank:

NIGHTLY THOUGHTS CONTINUED

Classes I Took Today (Answer If Applicable):

I Noticed:

What Parts Of My Body Feel Sore Today?

I No Longer Complain About:

What Felt Good Today?

What Tried To Discourage Me Today From Working Out?

What Did Not Feel Good Today?

I Took Advantage Of:

What Was A Challenge For Me Today?

I Am Progressing Towards:

I Am Working Through:

NEW BODY THIS MORNING

Date: Mood:

Today's Declaration:

My Body Is:

My Body Feels:

I Thank God For:

Today I Will Focus On:

My Exercise Goal For Today:

Today's Self-Talk:

MY NEW BODY - NIGHTLY THOUGHTS

Date:

IF I DID NOT WORK OUT TODAY
(FILL OUT THE FOLLOWING)....

How Did I Relax My Body Today?

Today I Allowed Myself:

What Changes Am I Starting To Notice?

Who Tried To Discourage Me From
Working Out Today?

IF I WORKED OUT TODAY
(FILL OUT THE FOLLOWING)....

Work Out Time:

Equipment That I Used Today:

Length Of Time Spent Working Out:

While Working Out Today, I Listened To:

My Exercise Heart Rate:

Did I Have A Workout Partner/Trainer Today
And If The Answer Is Yes, Who Was It?

My Heart Rate Resting:

I Motivated Myself By:

Today I Ate:

My Workout Today Consisted Of:

Today I Drank:

NIGHTLY THOUGHTS CONTINUED

Classes I Took Today (Answer If Applicable):

I Noticed:

What Parts Of My Body Feel Sore Today?

I No Longer Complain About:

What Felt Good Today?

What Tried To Discourage Me Today From Working Out?

What Did Not Feel Good Today?

I Took Advantage Of:

What Was A Challenge For Me Today?

I Am Progressing Towards:

I Am Working Through:

NEW BODY THIS MORNING

Date: Mood:

Today's Declaration:

My Body Is:

My Body Feels:

I Thank God For:

Today I Will Focus On:

My Exercise Goal For Today:

Today's Self-Talk:

MY NEW BODY - NIGHTLY THOUGHTS

Date:

IF I DID NOT WORK OUT TODAY
(FILL OUT THE FOLLOWING)....

How Did I Relax My Body Today?

Today I Allowed Myself:

What Changes Am I Starting To Notice?

Who Tried To Discourage Me From Working Out Today?

IF I WORKED OUT TODAY
(FILL OUT THE FOLLOWING)....

Work Out Time:

Equipment That I Used Today:

Length Of Time Spent Working Out:

While Working Out Today, I Listened To:

My Exercise Heart Rate:

Did I Have A Workout Partner/Trainer Today And If The Answer Is Yes, Who Was It?

My Heart Rate Resting:

I Motivated Myself By:

Today I Ate:

My Workout Today Consisted Of:

Today I Drank:

NIGHTLY THOUGHTS CONTINUED

Classes I Took Today (Answer If Applicable):

I Noticed:

What Parts Of My Body Feel Sore Today?

I No Longer Complain About:

What Felt Good Today?

What Tried To Discourage Me Today From Working Out?

What Did Not Feel Good Today?

I Took Advantage Of:

What Was A Challenge For Me Today?

I Am Progressing Towards:

I Am Working Through:

PERSONAL THOUGHTS

I LOOK GREAT.

NEW BODY THIS MORNING

Date: Mood:

Today's Declaration:

My Body Is:

My Body Feels:

I Thank God For:

Today I Will Focus On:

My Exercise Goal For Today:

Today's Self-Talk:

MY NEW BODY - NIGHTLY THOUGHTS

Date:

IF I DID NOT WORK OUT TODAY
(FILL OUT THE FOLLOWING)....

How Did I Relax My Body Today?

Today I Allowed Myself:

What Changes Am I Starting To Notice?

Who Tried To Discourage Me From
Working Out Today?

IF I WORKED OUT TODAY
(FILL OUT THE FOLLOWING)....

Work Out Time:

Equipment That I Used Today:

Length Of Time Spent Working Out:

While Working Out Today, I Listened To:

My Exercise Heart Rate:

Did I Have A Workout Partner/Trainer Today
And If The Answer Is Yes, Who Was It?

My Heart Rate Resting:

I Motivated Myself By:

Today I Ate:

My Workout Today Consisted Of:

Today I Drank:

NIGHTLY THOUGHTS CONTINUED

Classes I Took Today (Answer If Applicable):

I Noticed:

What Parts Of My Body Feel Sore Today?

I No Longer Complain About:

What Felt Good Today?

What Tried To Discourage Me Today From Working Out?

What Did Not Feel Good Today?

I Took Advantage Of:

What Was A Challenge For Me Today?

I Am Progressing Towards:

I Am Working Through:

NEW BODY THIS MORNING

Date: Mood:

Today's Declaration:

My Body Is:

My Body Feels:

I Thank God For:

Today I Will Focus On:

My Exercise Goal For Today:

Today's Self-Talk:

MY NEW BODY - NIGHTLY THOUGHTS

Date:

IF I DID NOT WORK OUT TODAY
(FILL OUT THE FOLLOWING)....

How Did I Relax My Body Today?

What Changes Am I Starting To Notice?

Today I Allowed Myself:

Who Tried To Discourage Me From Working Out Today?

IF I WORKED OUT TODAY
(FILL OUT THE FOLLOWING)....

Work Out Time:

Length Of Time Spent Working Out:

My Exercise Heart Rate:

My Heart Rate Resting:

I Motivated Myself By:

My Workout Today Consisted Of:

Equipment That I Used Today:

While Working Out Today, I Listened To:

Did I Have A Workout Partner/Trainer Today And If The Answer Is Yes, Who Was It?

Today I Ate:

Today I Drank:

NIGHTLY THOUGHTS CONTINUED

Classes I Took Today (Answer If Applicable):

I Noticed:

What Parts Of My Body Feel Sore Today?

I No Longer Complain About:

What Felt Good Today?

What Tried To Discourage Me Today From Working Out?

What Did Not Feel Good Today?

I Took Advantage Of:

What Was A Challenge For Me Today?

I Am Progressing Towards:

I Am Working Through:

NEW BODY THIS MORNING

Date: Mood:

Today's Declaration:

My Body Is:

My Body Feels:

I Thank God For:

Today I Will Focus On:

My Exercise Goal For Today:

Today's Self-Talk:

MY NEW BODY - NIGHTLY THOUGHTS

Date:

IF I DID NOT WORK OUT TODAY
(FILL OUT THE FOLLOWING)....

How Did I Relax My Body Today?

Today I Allowed Myself:

What Changes Am I Starting To Notice?

Who Tried To Discourage Me From Working Out Today?

IF I WORKED OUT TODAY
(FILL OUT THE FOLLOWING)....

Work Out Time:

Equipment That I Used Today:

Length Of Time Spent Working Out:

While Working Out Today, I Listened To:

My Exercise Heart Rate:

Did I Have A Workout Partner/Trainer Today And If The Answer Is Yes, Who Was It?

My Heart Rate Resting:

I Motivated Myself By:

Today I Ate:

My Workout Today Consisted Of:

Today I Drank:

NIGHTLY THOUGHTS CONTINUED

Classes I Took Today (Answer If Applicable):

I Noticed:

What Parts Of My Body Feel Sore Today?

I No Longer Complain About:

What Felt Good Today?

What Tried To Discourage Me Today From Working Out?

What Did Not Feel Good Today?

I Took Advantage Of:

What Was A Challenge For Me Today?

I Am Progressing Towards:

I Am Working Through:

I AM COMMITTED.

HEALTH AND FITNESS BOOKS AND WEBSITES THAT ARE MY GO TOS....

NEW BODY THIS MORNING

Date: Mood:

Today's Declaration:

My Body Is:

My Body Feels:

I Thank God For:

Today I Will Focus On:

My Exercise Goal For Today:

Today's Self-Talk:

MY NEW BODY – NIGHTLY THOUGHTS

Date:

IF I DID NOT WORK OUT TODAY
(FILL OUT THE FOLLOWING)....

How Did I Relax My Body Today?

Today I Allowed Myself:

What Changes Am I Starting To Notice?

Who Tried To Discourage Me From Working Out Today?

IF I WORKED OUT TODAY
(FILL OUT THE FOLLOWING)....

Work Out Time:

Equipment That I Used Today:

Length Of Time Spent Working Out:

While Working Out Today, I Listened To:

My Exercise Heart Rate:

Did I Have A Workout Partner/Trainer Today And If The Answer Is Yes, Who Was It?

My Heart Rate Resting:

I Motivated Myself By:

Today I Ate:

My Workout Today Consisted Of:

Today I Drank:

NIGHTLY THOUGHTS CONTINUED

Classes I Took Today (Answer If Applicable):

I Noticed:

What Parts Of My Body Feel Sore Today?

I No Longer Complain About:

What Felt Good Today?

What Tried To Discourage Me Today From Working Out?

What Did Not Feel Good Today?

I Took Advantage Of:

What Was A Challenge For Me Today?

I Am Progressing Towards:

I Am Working Through:

NEW BODY THIS MORNING

Date: Mood:

Today's Declaration:

My Body Is:

My Body Feels:

I Thank God For:

Today I Will Focus On:

My Exercise Goal For Today:

Today's Self-Talk:

MY NEW BODY - NIGHTLY THOUGHTS

Date:

IF I DID NOT WORK OUT TODAY
(FILL OUT THE FOLLOWING)....

How Did I Relax My Body Today?

Today I Allowed Myself:

What Changes Am I Starting To Notice?

Who Tried To Discourage Me From Working Out Today?

IF I WORKED OUT TODAY
(FILL OUT THE FOLLOWING)....

Work Out Time:

Equipment That I Used Today:

Length Of Time Spent Working Out:

While Working Out Today, I Listened To:

My Exercise Heart Rate:

Did I Have A Workout Partner/Trainer Today And If The Answer Is Yes, Who Was It?

My Heart Rate Resting:

I Motivated Myself By:

Today I Ate:

My Workout Today Consisted Of:

Today I Drank:

NIGHTLY THOUGHTS CONTINUED

Classes I Took Today (Answer If Applicable):

I Noticed:

What Parts Of My Body Feel Sore Today?

I No Longer Complain About:

What Felt Good Today?

What Tried To Discourage Me Today From Working Out?

What Did Not Feel Good Today?

I Took Advantage Of:

What Was A Challenge For Me Today?

I Am Progressing Towards:

I Am Working Through:

NEW BODY THIS MORNING

Date: Mood:

Today's Declaration:

My Body Is:

My Body Feels:

I Thank God For:

Today I Will Focus On:

My Exercise Goal For Today:

Today's Self-Talk:

MY NEW BODY - NIGHTLY THOUGHTS

Date:

IF I DID NOT WORK OUT TODAY
(FILL OUT THE FOLLOWING)....

How Did I Relax My Body Today?

Today I Allowed Myself:

What Changes Am I Starting To Notice?

Who Tried To Discourage Me From Working Out Today?

IF I WORKED OUT TODAY
(FILL OUT THE FOLLOWING)....

Work Out Time:

Equipment That I Used Today:

Length Of Time Spent Working Out:

While Working Out Today, I Listened To:

My Exercise Heart Rate:

Did I Have A Workout Partner/Trainer Today And If The Answer Is Yes, Who Was It?

My Heart Rate Resting:

I Motivated Myself By:

Today I Ate:

My Workout Today Consisted Of:

Today I Drank:

NIGHTLY THOUGHTS CONTINUED

Classes I Took Today (Answer If Applicable):

I Noticed:

What Parts Of My Body Feel Sore Today?

I No Longer Complain About:

What Felt Good Today?

What Tried To Discourage Me Today From Working Out?

What Did Not Feel Good Today?

I Took Advantage Of:

What Was A Challenge For Me Today?

I Am Progressing Towards:

I Am Working Through:

PUT IN THAT EFFORT.

NO SUCH THING AS TOMORROW. ALL I HAVE IS RIGHT NOW.

NEW BODY THIS MORNING

Date: Mood:

Today's Declaration:

My Body Is:

My Body Feels:

I Thank God For:

Today I Will Focus On:

My Exercise Goal For Today:

Today's Self-Talk:

MY NEW BODY - NIGHTLY THOUGHTS

Date:

IF I DID NOT WORK OUT TODAY
(FILL OUT THE FOLLOWING)....

How Did I Relax My Body Today?

Today I Allowed Myself:

What Changes Am I Starting To Notice?

Who Tried To Discourage Me From Working Out Today?

IF I WORKED OUT TODAY
(FILL OUT THE FOLLOWING)....

Work Out Time:

Equipment That I Used Today:

Length Of Time Spent Working Out:

While Working Out Today, I Listened To:

My Exercise Heart Rate:

Did I Have A Workout Partner/Trainer Today And If The Answer Is Yes, Who Was It?

My Heart Rate Resting:

I Motivated Myself By:

Today I Ate:

My Workout Today Consisted Of:

Today I Drank:

NIGHTLY THOUGHTS CONTINUED

Classes I Took Today (Answer If Applicable):

I Noticed:

What Parts Of My Body Feel Sore Today?

I No Longer Complain About:

What Felt Good Today?

What Tried To Discourage Me Today From Working Out?

What Did Not Feel Good Today?

I Took Advantage Of:

What Was A Challenge For Me Today?

I Am Progressing Towards:

I Am Working Through:

NEW BODY THIS MORNING

Date:

Mood:

Today's Declaration:

My Body Is:

My Body Feels:

I Thank God For:

Today I Will Focus On:

My Exercise Goal For Today:

Today's Self-Talk:

MY NEW BODY - NIGHTLY THOUGHTS

Date:

IF I DID NOT WORK OUT TODAY
(FILL OUT THE FOLLOWING)....

How Did I Relax My Body Today?

Today I Allowed Myself:

What Changes Am I Starting To Notice?

Who Tried To Discourage Me From Working Out Today?

IF I WORKED OUT TODAY
(FILL OUT THE FOLLOWING)....

Work Out Time:

Equipment That I Used Today:

Length Of Time Spent Working Out:

While Working Out Today, I Listened To:

My Exercise Heart Rate:

Did I Have A Workout Partner/Trainer Today And If The Answer Is Yes, Who Was It?

My Heart Rate Resting:

I Motivated Myself By:

Today I Ate:

My Workout Today Consisted Of:

Today I Drank:

NIGHTLY THOUGHTS CONTINUED

Classes I Took Today (Answer If Applicable):

I Noticed:

What Parts Of My Body Feel Sore Today?

I No Longer Complain About:

What Felt Good Today?

What Tried To Discourage Me Today From Working Out?

What Did Not Feel Good Today?

I Took Advantage Of:

What Was A Challenge For Me Today?

I Am Progressing Towards:

I Am Working Through:

NEW BODY THIS MORNING

Date: Mood:

Today's Declaration:

My Body Is:

My Body Feels:

I Thank God For:

Today I Will Focus On:

My Exercise Goal For Today:

Today's Self-Talk:

MY NEW BODY - NIGHTLY THOUGHTS

Date:

IF I DID NOT WORK OUT TODAY
(FILL OUT THE FOLLOWING)....

How Did I Relax My Body Today?

Today I Allowed Myself:

What Changes Am I Starting To Notice?

Who Tried To Discourage Me From Working Out Today?

IF I WORKED OUT TODAY
(FILL OUT THE FOLLOWING)....

Work Out Time:

Equipment That I Used Today:

Length Of Time Spent Working Out:

While Working Out Today, I Listened To:

My Exercise Heart Rate:

Did I Have A Workout Partner/Trainer Today And If The Answer Is Yes, Who Was It?

My Heart Rate Resting:

I Motivated Myself By:

Today I Ate:

My Workout Today Consisted Of:

Today I Drank:

NIGHTLY THOUGHTS CONTINUED

Classes I Took Today (Answer If Applicable):

I Noticed:

What Parts Of My Body Feel Sore Today?

I No Longer Complain About:

What Felt Good Today?

What Tried To Discourage Me Today From Working Out?

What Did Not Feel Good Today?

I Took Advantage Of:

What Was A Challenge For Me Today?

I Am Progressing Towards:

I Am Working Through:

IT DOES NOT MATTER WHAT ANYBODY SAYS. I WILL REACH MY GOALS.

I AM A WINNER.

NEW BODY THIS MORNING

Date:

Mood:

Today's Declaration:

My Body Is:

My Body Feels:

I Thank God For:

Today I Will Focus On:

My Exercise Goal For Today:

Today's Self-Talk:

MY NEW BODY - NIGHTLY THOUGHTS

Date:

IF I DID NOT WORK OUT TODAY
(FILL OUT THE FOLLOWING)....

How Did I Relax My Body Today?

Today I Allowed Myself:

What Changes Am I Starting To Notice?

Who Tried To Discourage Me From Working Out Today?

IF I WORKED OUT TODAY
(FILL OUT THE FOLLOWING)....

Work Out Time:

Equipment That I Used Today:

Length Of Time Spent Working Out:

While Working Out Today, I Listened To:

My Exercise Heart Rate:

Did I Have A Workout Partner/Trainer Today And If The Answer Is Yes, Who Was It?

My Heart Rate Resting:

I Motivated Myself By:

Today I Ate:

My Workout Today Consisted Of:

Today I Drank:

NIGHTLY THOUGHTS CONTINUED

Classes I Took Today (Answer If Applicable):

I Noticed:

What Parts Of My Body Feel Sore Today?

I No Longer Complain About:

What Felt Good Today?

What Tried To Discourage Me Today From Working Out?

What Did Not Feel Good Today?

I Took Advantage Of:

What Was A Challenge For Me Today?

I Am Progressing Towards:

I Am Working Through:

NEW BODY THIS MORNING

Date: Mood:

Today's Declaration:

My Body Is:

My Body Feels:

I Thank God For:

Today I Will Focus On:

My Exercise Goal For Today:

Today's Self-Talk:

MY NEW BODY - NIGHTLY THOUGHTS

Date:

IF I DID NOT WORK OUT TODAY
(FILL OUT THE FOLLOWING)....

How Did I Relax My Body Today?

Today I Allowed Myself:

What Changes Am I Starting To Notice?

Who Tried To Discourage Me From
Working Out Today?

IF I WORKED OUT TODAY
(FILL OUT THE FOLLOWING)....

Work Out Time:

Equipment That I Used Today:

Length Of Time Spent Working Out:

While Working Out Today, I Listened To:

My Exercise Heart Rate:

Did I Have A Workout Partner/Trainer Today
And If The Answer Is Yes, Who Was It?

My Heart Rate Resting:

I Motivated Myself By:

Today I Ate:

My Workout Today Consisted Of:

Today I Drank:

174

NIGHTLY THOUGHTS CONTINUED

Classes I Took Today (Answer If Applicable):

I Noticed:

What Parts Of My Body Feel Sore Today?

I No Longer Complain About:

What Felt Good Today?

What Tried To Discourage Me Today From Working Out?

What Did Not Feel Good Today?

I Took Advantage Of:

What Was A Challenge For Me Today?

I Am Progressing Towards:

I Am Working Through:

NEW BODY THIS MORNING

Date: Mood:

Today's Declaration:

My Body Is:

My Body Feels:

I Thank God For:

Today I Will Focus On:

My Exercise Goal For Today:

Today's Self-Talk:

MY NEW BODY - NIGHTLY THOUGHTS

Date:

IF I DID NOT WORK OUT TODAY
(FILL OUT THE FOLLOWING)....

How Did I Relax My Body Today?

Today I Allowed Myself:

What Changes Am I Starting To Notice?

Who Tried To Discourage Me From Working Out Today?

IF I WORKED OUT TODAY
(FILL OUT THE FOLLOWING)....

Work Out Time:

Equipment That I Used Today:

Length Of Time Spent Working Out:

While Working Out Today, I Listened To:

My Exercise Heart Rate:

Did I Have A Workout Partner/Trainer Today And If The Answer Is Yes, Who Was It?

My Heart Rate Resting:

I Motivated Myself By:

Today I Ate:

My Workout Today Consisted Of:

Today I Drank:

NIGHTLY THOUGHTS CONTINUED

Classes I Took Today (Answer If Applicable):

I Noticed:

What Parts Of My Body Feel Sore Today?

I No Longer Complain About:

What Felt Good Today?

What Tried To Discourage Me Today From Working Out?

What Did Not Feel Good Today?

I Took Advantage Of:

What Was A Challenge For Me Today?

I Am Progressing Towards:

I Am Working Through:

PERSONAL THOUGHTS

I WILL ACHIEVE EVERY GOAL I SET OUT FOR MYSELF.

NEW BODY THIS MORNING

Date: Mood:

Today's Declaration:

My Body Is:

My Body Feels:

I Thank God For:

Today I Will Focus On:

My Exercise Goal For Today:

Today's Self-Talk:

MY NEW BODY - NIGHTLY THOUGHTS

Date:

IF I DID NOT WORK OUT TODAY
(FILL OUT THE FOLLOWING)....

How Did I Relax My Body Today?

Today I Allowed Myself:

What Changes Am I Starting To Notice?

Who Tried To Discourage Me From
Working Out Today?

IF I WORKED OUT TODAY
(FILL OUT THE FOLLOWING)....

Work Out Time:

Equipment That I Used Today:

Length Of Time Spent Working Out:

While Working Out Today, I Listened To:

My Exercise Heart Rate:

Did I Have A Workout Partner/Trainer Today
And If The Answer Is Yes, Who Was It?

My Heart Rate Resting:

I Motivated Myself By:

Today I Ate:

My Workout Today Consisted Of:

Today I Drank:

NIGHTLY THOUGHTS CONTINUED

Classes I Took Today (Answer If Applicable):

I Noticed:

What Parts Of My Body Feel Sore Today?

I No Longer Complain About:

What Felt Good Today?

What Tried To Discourage Me Today From Working Out?

What Did Not Feel Good Today?

I Took Advantage Of:

What Was A Challenge For Me Today?

I Am Progressing Towards:

I Am Working Through:

NEW BODY THIS MORNING

Date: Mood:

Today's Declaration:

My Body Is:

My Body Feels:

I Thank God For:

Today I Will Focus On:

My Exercise Goal For Today:

Today's Self-Talk:

184

MY NEW BODY - NIGHTLY THOUGHTS

Date:

IF I DID NOT WORK OUT TODAY
(FILL OUT THE FOLLOWING)....

How Did I Relax My Body Today?

Today I Allowed Myself:

What Changes Am I Starting To Notice?

Who Tried To Discourage Me From Working Out Today?

IF I WORKED OUT TODAY
(FILL OUT THE FOLLOWING)....

Work Out Time:

Equipment That I Used Today:

Length Of Time Spent Working Out:

While Working Out Today, I Listened To:

My Exercise Heart Rate:

Did I Have A Workout Partner/Trainer Today And If The Answer Is Yes, Who Was It?

My Heart Rate Resting:

I Motivated Myself By:

Today I Ate:

My Workout Today Consisted Of:

Today I Drank:

NIGHTLY THOUGHTS CONTINUED

Classes I Took Today (Answer If Applicable):

I Noticed:

What Parts Of My Body Feel Sore Today?

I No Longer Complain About:

What Felt Good Today?

What Tried To Discourage Me Today From Working Out?

What Did Not Feel Good Today?

I Took Advantage Of:

What Was A Challenge For Me Today?

I Am Progressing Towards:

I Am Working Through:

NEW BODY THIS MORNING

Date: Mood:

Today's Declaration:

My Body Is:

My Body Feels:

I Thank God For:

Today I Will Focus On:

My Exercise Goal For Today:

Today's Self-Talk:

MY NEW BODY - NIGHTLY THOUGHTS

Date:

IF I DID NOT WORK OUT TODAY
(FILL OUT THE FOLLOWING)....

How Did I Relax My Body Today?

Today I Allowed Myself:

What Changes Am I Starting To Notice?

Who Tried To Discourage Me From Working Out Today?

IF I WORKED OUT TODAY
(FILL OUT THE FOLLOWING)....

Work Out Time:

Equipment That I Used Today:

Length Of Time Spent Working Out:

While Working Out Today, I Listened To:

My Exercise Heart Rate:

Did I Have A Workout Partner/Trainer Today And If The Answer Is Yes, Who Was It?

My Heart Rate Resting:

I Motivated Myself By:

Today I Ate:

My Workout Today Consisted Of:

Today I Drank:

NIGHTLY THOUGHTS CONTINUED

Classes I Took Today (Answer If Applicable):

I Noticed:

What Parts Of My Body Feel Sore Today?

I No Longer Complain About:

What Felt Good Today?

What Tried To Discourage Me Today From Working Out?

What Did Not Feel Good Today?

I Took Advantage Of:

What Was A Challenge For Me Today?

I Am Progressing Towards:

I Am Working Through:

I AM MAKING MYSELF PROUD.

WHAT KEEPS ME MOTIVATED?

NEW BODY THIS MORNING

Date: Mood:

Today's Declaration:

My Body Is:

My Body Feels:

I Thank God For:

Today I Will Focus On:

My Exercise Goal For Today:

Today's Self-Talk:

MY NEW BODY - NIGHTLY THOUGHTS

Date:

IF I DID NOT WORK OUT TODAY
(FILL OUT THE FOLLOWING)....

How Did I Relax My Body Today?

Today I Allowed Myself:

What Changes Am I Starting To Notice?

Who Tried To Discourage Me From
Working Out Today?

IF I WORKED OUT TODAY
(FILL OUT THE FOLLOWING)....

Work Out Time:

Equipment That I Used Today:

Length Of Time Spent Working Out:

While Working Out Today, I Listened To:

My Exercise Heart Rate:

Did I Have A Workout Partner/Trainer Today
And If The Answer Is Yes, Who Was It?

My Heart Rate Resting:

I Motivated Myself By:

Today I Ate:

My Workout Today Consisted Of:

Today I Drank:

NIGHTLY THOUGHTS CONTINUED

Classes I Took Today (Answer If Applicable):

I Noticed:

What Parts Of My Body Feel Sore Today?

I No Longer Complain About:

What Felt Good Today?

What Tried To Discourage Me Today From Working Out?

What Did Not Feel Good Today?

I Took Advantage Of:

What Was A Challenge For Me Today?

I Am Progressing Towards:

I Am Working Through:

NEW BODY THIS MORNING

Date: Mood:

Today's Declaration:

My Body Is:

My Body Feels:

I Thank God For:

Today I Will Focus On:

My Exercise Goal For Today:

Today's Self-Talk:

MY NEW BODY - NIGHTLY THOUGHTS

Date:

IF I DID NOT WORK OUT TODAY
(FILL OUT THE FOLLOWING)....

How Did I Relax My Body Today?

Today I Allowed Myself:

What Changes Am I Starting To Notice?

Who Tried To Discourage Me From Working Out Today?

IF I WORKED OUT TODAY
(FILL OUT THE FOLLOWING)....

Work Out Time:

Equipment That I Used Today:

Length Of Time Spent Working Out:

While Working Out Today, I Listened To:

My Exercise Heart Rate:

Did I Have A Workout Partner/Trainer Today And If The Answer Is Yes, Who Was It?

My Heart Rate Resting:

I Motivated Myself By:

Today I Ate:

My Workout Today Consisted Of:

Today I Drank:

NIGHTLY THOUGHTS CONTINUED

Classes I Took Today (Answer If Applicable):

I Noticed:

What Parts Of My Body Feel Sore Today?

I No Longer Complain About:

What Felt Good Today?

What Tried To Discourage Me Today From Working Out?

What Did Not Feel Good Today?

I Took Advantage Of:

What Was A Challenge For Me Today?

I Am Progressing Towards:

I Am Working Through:

NEW BODY THIS MORNING

Date: Mood:

Today's Declaration:

My Body Is:

My Body Feels:

I Thank God For:

Today I Will Focus On:

My Exercise Goal For Today:

Today's Self-Talk:

MY NEW BODY - NIGHTLY THOUGHTS

Date:

IF I DID NOT WORK OUT TODAY
(FILL OUT THE FOLLOWING)....

How Did I Relax My Body Today?

Today I Allowed Myself:

What Changes Am I Starting To Notice?

Who Tried To Discourage Me From
Working Out Today?

IF I WORKED OUT TODAY
(FILL OUT THE FOLLOWING)....

Work Out Time:

Equipment That I Used Today:

Length Of Time Spent Working Out:

While Working Out Today, I Listened To:

My Exercise Heart Rate:

Did I Have A Workout Partner/Trainer Today
And If The Answer Is Yes, Who Was It?

My Heart Rate Resting:

I Motivated Myself By:

Today I Ate:

My Workout Today Consisted Of:

Today I Drank:

NIGHTLY THOUGHTS CONTINUED

Classes I Took Today (Answer If Applicable):

I Noticed:

What Parts Of My Body Feel Sore Today?

I No Longer Complain About:

What Felt Good Today?

What Tried To Discourage Me Today From Working Out?

What Did Not Feel Good Today?

I Took Advantage Of:

What Was A Challenge For Me Today?

I Am Progressing Towards:

I Am Working Through:

PERSONAL THOUGHTS

JUST BECAUSE IT DOES NOT FEEL GOOD TODAY, DOES NOT MEAN I WILL NOT BE PROUD OF MY DECISION TOMORROW.

NEW BODY THIS MORNING

Date: Mood:

Today's Declaration:

My Body Is:

My Body Feels:

I Thank God For:

Today I Will Focus On:

My Exercise Goal For Today:

Today's Self-Talk:

MY NEW BODY - NIGHTLY THOUGHTS

Date:

IF I DID NOT WORK OUT TODAY
(FILL OUT THE FOLLOWING)....

How Did I Relax My Body Today?

What Changes Am I Starting To Notice?

Today I Allowed Myself:

Who Tried To Discourage Me From Working Out Today?

IF I WORKED OUT TODAY
(FILL OUT THE FOLLOWING)....

Work Out Time:

Length Of Time Spent Working Out:

My Exercise Heart Rate:

My Heart Rate Resting:

I Motivated Myself By:

My Workout Today Consisted Of:

Equipment That I Used Today:

While Working Out Today, I Listened To:

Did I Have A Workout Partner/Trainer Today And If The Answer Is Yes, Who Was It?

Today I Ate:

Today I Drank:

NIGHTLY THOUGHTS CONTINUED

Classes I Took Today (Answer If Applicable):

I Noticed:

What Parts Of My Body Feel Sore Today?

I No Longer Complain About:

What Felt Good Today?

What Tried To Discourage Me Today From Working Out?

What Did Not Feel Good Today?

I Took Advantage Of:

What Was A Challenge For Me Today?

I Am Progressing Towards:

I Am Working Through:

NEW BODY THIS MORNING

Date: Mood:

Today's Declaration:

My Body Is:

My Body Feels:

I Thank God For:

Today I Will Focus On:

My Exercise Goal For Today:

Today's Self-Talk:

MY NEW BODY - NIGHTLY THOUGHTS

Date:

IF I DID NOT WORK OUT TODAY
(FILL OUT THE FOLLOWING)....

How Did I Relax My Body Today?

Today I Allowed Myself:

What Changes Am I Starting To Notice?

Who Tried To Discourage Me From Working Out Today?

IF I WORKED OUT TODAY
(FILL OUT THE FOLLOWING)....

Work Out Time:

Equipment That I Used Today:

Length Of Time Spent Working Out:

While Working Out Today, I Listened To:

My Exercise Heart Rate:

Did I Have A Workout Partner/Trainer Today And If The Answer Is Yes, Who Was It?

My Heart Rate Resting:

I Motivated Myself By:

Today I Ate:

My Workout Today Consisted Of:

Today I Drank:

NIGHTLY THOUGHTS CONTINUED

Classes I Took Today (Answer If Applicable):

I Noticed:

What Parts Of My Body Feel Sore Today?

I No Longer Complain About:

What Felt Good Today?

What Tried To Discourage Me Today From Working Out?

What Did Not Feel Good Today?

I Took Advantage Of:

What Was A Challenge For Me Today?

I Am Progressing Towards:

I Am Working Through:

NEW BODY THIS MORNING

Date: Mood:

Today's Declaration:

My Body Is:

My Body Feels:

I Thank God For:

Today I Will Focus On:

My Exercise Goal For Today:

Today's Self-Talk:

MY NEW BODY - NIGHTLY THOUGHTS

Date:

IF I DID NOT WORK OUT TODAY
(FILL OUT THE FOLLOWING)....

How Did I Relax My Body Today?

Today I Allowed Myself:

What Changes Am I Starting To Notice?

Who Tried To Discourage Me From
Working Out Today?

IF I WORKED OUT TODAY
(FILL OUT THE FOLLOWING)....

Work Out Time:

Equipment That I Used Today:

Length Of Time Spent Working Out:

While Working Out Today, I Listened To:

My Exercise Heart Rate:

Did I Have A Workout Partner/Trainer Today
And If The Answer Is Yes, Who Was It?

My Heart Rate Resting:

I Motivated Myself By:

Today I Ate:

My Workout Today Consisted Of:

Today I Drank:

NIGHTLY THOUGHTS CONTINUED

Classes I Took Today (Answer If Applicable):

I Noticed:

What Parts Of My Body Feel Sore Today?

I No Longer Complain About:

What Felt Good Today?

What Tried To Discourage Me Today From Working Out?

What Did Not Feel Good Today?

I Took Advantage Of:

What Was A Challenge For Me Today?

I Am Progressing Towards:

I Am Working Through:

THE BATTLE IS IN MY MIND THEN THE GYM.

MY ROUTINE AFTER A WORKOUT IS....

NEW BODY THIS MORNING

Date: Mood:

Today's Declaration:

My Body Is:

My Body Feels:

I Thank God For:

Today I Will Focus On:

My Exercise Goal For Today:

Today's Self-Talk:

MY NEW BODY - NIGHTLY THOUGHTS

Date:

IF I DID NOT WORK OUT TODAY
(FILL OUT THE FOLLOWING)....

How Did I Relax My Body Today?

Today I Allowed Myself:

What Changes Am I Starting To Notice?

Who Tried To Discourage Me From
Working Out Today?

IF I WORKED OUT TODAY
(FILL OUT THE FOLLOWING)....

Work Out Time:

Equipment That I Used Today:

Length Of Time Spent Working Out:

While Working Out Today, I Listened To:

My Exercise Heart Rate:

Did I Have A Workout Partner/Trainer Today
And If The Answer Is Yes, Who Was It?

My Heart Rate Resting:

I Motivated Myself By:

Today I Ate:

My Workout Today Consisted Of:

Today I Drank:

NIGHTLY THOUGHTS CONTINUED

Classes I Took Today (Answer If Applicable):

I Noticed:

What Parts Of My Body Feel Sore Today?

I No Longer Complain About:

What Felt Good Today?

What Tried To Discourage Me Today From Working Out?

What Did Not Feel Good Today?

I Took Advantage Of:

What Was A Challenge For Me Today?

I Am Progressing Towards:

I Am Working Through:

NEW BODY THIS MORNING

Date: Mood:

Today's Declaration:

My Body Is:

My Body Feels:

I Thank God For:

Today I Will Focus On:

My Exercise Goal For Today:

Today's Self-Talk:

MY NEW BODY - NIGHTLY THOUGHTS

Date:

IF I DID NOT WORK OUT TODAY
(FILL OUT THE FOLLOWING)....

How Did I Relax My Body Today?

Today I Allowed Myself:

What Changes Am I Starting To Notice?

Who Tried To Discourage Me From Working Out Today?

IF I WORKED OUT TODAY
(FILL OUT THE FOLLOWING)....

Work Out Time:

Equipment That I Used Today:

Length Of Time Spent Working Out:

While Working Out Today, I Listened To:

My Exercise Heart Rate:

Did I Have A Workout Partner/Trainer Today And If The Answer Is Yes, Who Was It?

My Heart Rate Resting:

I Motivated Myself By:

Today I Ate:

My Workout Today Consisted Of:

Today I Drank:

NIGHTLY THOUGHTS CONTINUED

Classes I Took Today (Answer If Applicable):

I Noticed:

What Parts Of My Body Feel Sore Today?

I No Longer Complain About:

What Felt Good Today?

What Tried To Discourage Me Today From Working Out?

What Did Not Feel Good Today?

I Took Advantage Of:

What Was A Challenge For Me Today?

I Am Progressing Towards:

I Am Working Through:

NEW BODY THIS MORNING

Date: Mood:

Today's Declaration:

My Body Is:

My Body Feels:

I Thank God For:

Today I Will Focus On:

My Exercise Goal For Today:

Today's Self-Talk:

MY NEW BODY - NIGHTLY THOUGHTS

Date:

IF I DID NOT WORK OUT TODAY
(FILL OUT THE FOLLOWING)....

How Did I Relax My Body Today?

Today I Allowed Myself:

What Changes Am I Starting To Notice?

Who Tried To Discourage Me From
Working Out Today?

IF I WORKED OUT TODAY
(FILL OUT THE FOLLOWING)....

Work Out Time:

Equipment That I Used Today:

Length Of Time Spent Working Out:

While Working Out Today, I Listened To:

My Exercise Heart Rate:

Did I Have A Workout Partner/Trainer Today
And If The Answer Is Yes, Who Was It?

My Heart Rate Resting:

I Motivated Myself By:

Today I Ate:

My Workout Today Consisted Of:

Today I Drank:

NIGHTLY THOUGHTS CONTINUED

Classes I Took Today (Answer If Applicable):

I Noticed:

What Parts Of My Body Feel Sore Today?

I No Longer Complain About:

What Felt Good Today?

What Tried To Discourage Me Today From Working Out?

What Did Not Feel Good Today?

I Took Advantage Of:

What Was A Challenge For Me Today?

I Am Progressing Towards:

I Am Working Through:

PERSONAL THOUGHTS

STAY POSITIVE. STAY FOCUSED.

NEW BODY THIS MORNING

Date: Mood:

Today's Declaration:

My Body Is:

My Body Feels:

I Thank God For:

Today I Will Focus On:

My Exercise Goal For Today:

Today's Self-Talk:

MY NEW BODY - NIGHTLY THOUGHTS

Date:

IF I DID NOT WORK OUT TODAY
(FILL OUT THE FOLLOWING)....

How Did I Relax My Body Today?

Today I Allowed Myself:

What Changes Am I Starting To Notice?

Who Tried To Discourage Me From Working Out Today?

IF I WORKED OUT TODAY
(FILL OUT THE FOLLOWING)....

Work Out Time:

Equipment That I Used Today:

Length Of Time Spent Working Out:

While Working Out Today, I Listened To:

My Exercise Heart Rate:

Did I Have A Workout Partner/Trainer Today And If The Answer Is Yes, Who Was It?

My Heart Rate Resting:

I Motivated Myself By:

Today I Ate:

My Workout Today Consisted Of:

Today I Drank:

Classes I Took Today (Answer If Applicable):

I Noticed:

What Parts Of My Body Feel Sore Today?

I No Longer Complain About:

What Felt Good Today?

What Tried To Discourage Me Today From Working Out?

What Did Not Feel Good Today?

I Took Advantage Of:

What Was A Challenge For Me Today?

I Am Progressing Towards:

I Am Working Through:

NEW BODY THIS MORNING

Date: Mood:

Today's Declaration:

My Body Is:

My Body Feels:

I Thank God For:

Today I Will Focus On:

My Exercise Goal For Today:

Today's Self-Talk:

228

MY NEW BODY - NIGHTLY THOUGHTS

Date:

IF I DID NOT WORK OUT TODAY
(FILL OUT THE FOLLOWING)....

How Did I Relax My Body Today?

Today I Allowed Myself:

What Changes Am I Starting To Notice?

Who Tried To Discourage Me From
Working Out Today?

IF I WORKED OUT TODAY
(FILL OUT THE FOLLOWING)....

Work Out Time:

Equipment That I Used Today:

Length Of Time Spent Working Out:

While Working Out Today, I Listened To:

My Exercise Heart Rate:

Did I Have A Workout Partner/Trainer Today
And If The Answer Is Yes, Who Was It?

My Heart Rate Resting:

I Motivated Myself By:

Today I Ate:

My Workout Today Consisted Of:

Today I Drank:

Classes I Took Today (Answer If Applicable):

I Noticed:

What Parts Of My Body Feel Sore Today?

I No Longer Complain About:

What Felt Good Today?

What Tried To Discourage Me Today From Working Out?

What Did Not Feel Good Today?

I Took Advantage Of:

What Was A Challenge For Me Today?

I Am Progressing Towards:

I Am Working Through:

NEW BODY THIS MORNING

Date: Mood:

Today's Declaration:

My Body Is:

My Body Feels:

I Thank God For:

Today I Will Focus On:

My Exercise Goal For Today:

Today's Self-Talk:

MY NEW BODY - NIGHTLY THOUGHTS

Date:

IF I DID NOT WORK OUT TODAY
(FILL OUT THE FOLLOWING)....

How Did I Relax My Body Today?

Today I Allowed Myself:

What Changes Am I Starting To Notice?

Who Tried To Discourage Me From Working Out Today?

IF I WORKED OUT TODAY
(FILL OUT THE FOLLOWING)....

Work Out Time:

Equipment That I Used Today:

Length Of Time Spent Working Out:

While Working Out Today, I Listened To:

My Exercise Heart Rate:

Did I Have A Workout Partner/Trainer Today And If The Answer Is Yes, Who Was It?

My Heart Rate Resting:

I Motivated Myself By:

Today I Ate:

My Workout Today Consisted Of:

Today I Drank:

NIGHTLY THOUGHTS CONTINUED

Classes I Took Today (Answer If Applicable):

I Noticed:

What Parts Of My Body Feel Sore Today?

I No Longer Complain About:

What Felt Good Today?

What Tried To Discourage Me Today From Working Out?

What Did Not Feel Good Today?

I Took Advantage Of:

What Was A Challenge For Me Today?

I Am Progressing Towards:

I Am Working Through:

THE FOCUS IS ON HEALTH.

A LIST OF MY GO TO HEALTHY MEALS ARE....

NEW BODY THIS MORNING

Date: Mood:

Today's Declaration:

My Body Is:

My Body Feels:

I Thank God For:

Today I Will Focus On:

My Exercise Goal For Today:

Today's Self-Talk:

MY NEW BODY - NIGHTLY THOUGHTS

Date:

IF I DID NOT WORK OUT TODAY
(FILL OUT THE FOLLOWING)....

How Did I Relax My Body Today?

Today I Allowed Myself:

What Changes Am I Starting To Notice?

Who Tried To Discourage Me From
Working Out Today?

IF I WORKED OUT TODAY
(FILL OUT THE FOLLOWING)....

Work Out Time:

Equipment That I Used Today:

Length Of Time Spent Working Out:

While Working Out Today, I Listened To:

My Exercise Heart Rate:

Did I Have A Workout Partner/Trainer Today
And If The Answer Is Yes, Who Was It?

My Heart Rate Resting:

I Motivated Myself By:

Today I Ate:

My Workout Today Consisted Of:

Today I Drank:

NIGHTLY THOUGHTS CONTINUED

Classes I Took Today (Answer If Applicable):

I Noticed:

What Parts Of My Body Feel Sore Today?

I No Longer Complain About:

What Felt Good Today?

What Tried To Discourage Me Today From Working Out?

What Did Not Feel Good Today?

I Took Advantage Of:

What Was A Challenge For Me Today?

I Am Progressing Towards:

I Am Working Through:

NEW BODY THIS MORNING

Date: Mood:

Today's Declaration:

My Body Is:

My Body Feels:

I Thank God For:

Today I Will Focus On:

My Exercise Goal For Today:

Today's Self-Talk:

MY NEW BODY - NIGHTLY THOUGHTS

Date:

IF I DID NOT WORK OUT TODAY
(FILL OUT THE FOLLOWING)....

How Did I Relax My Body Today?

Today I Allowed Myself:

What Changes Am I Starting To Notice?

Who Tried To Discourage Me From Working Out Today?

IF I WORKED OUT TODAY
(FILL OUT THE FOLLOWING)....

Work Out Time:

Equipment That I Used Today:

Length Of Time Spent Working Out:

While Working Out Today, I Listened To:

My Exercise Heart Rate:

Did I Have A Workout Partner/Trainer Today And If The Answer Is Yes, Who Was It?

My Heart Rate Resting:

I Motivated Myself By:

Today I Ate:

My Workout Today Consisted Of:

Today I Drank:

NIGHTLY THOUGHTS CONTINUED

Classes I Took Today (Answer If Applicable):

I Noticed:

What Parts Of My Body Feel Sore Today?

I No Longer Complain About:

What Felt Good Today?

What Tried To Discourage Me Today From Working Out?

What Did Not Feel Good Today?

I Took Advantage Of:

What Was A Challenge For Me Today?

I Am Progressing Towards:

I Am Working Through:

NEW BODY THIS MORNING

Date: Mood:

Today's Declaration:

My Body Is:

My Body Feels:

I Thank God For:

Today I Will Focus On:

My Exercise Goal For Today:

Today's Self-Talk:

MY NEW BODY - NIGHTLY THOUGHTS

Date:

IF I DID NOT WORK OUT TODAY
(FILL OUT THE FOLLOWING)....

How Did I Relax My Body Today?

Today I Allowed Myself:

What Changes Am I Starting To Notice?

Who Tried To Discourage Me From Working Out Today?

IF I WORKED OUT TODAY
(FILL OUT THE FOLLOWING)....

Work Out Time:

Equipment That I Used Today:

Length Of Time Spent Working Out:

While Working Out Today, I Listened To:

My Exercise Heart Rate:

Did I Have A Workout Partner/Trainer Today And If The Answer Is Yes, Who Was It?

My Heart Rate Resting:

I Motivated Myself By:

Today I Ate:

My Workout Today Consisted Of:

Today I Drank:

NIGHTLY THOUGHTS CONTINUED

Classes I Took Today (Answer If Applicable):

I Noticed:

What Parts Of My Body Feel Sore Today?

I No Longer Complain About:

What Felt Good Today?

What Tried To Discourage Me Today From Working Out?

What Did Not Feel Good Today?

I Took Advantage Of:

What Was A Challenge For Me Today?

I Am Progressing Towards:

I Am Working Through:

PERSONAL THOUGHTS

I AM LOVING THE RESULTS.

NEW BODY THIS MORNING

Date: Mood:

Today's Declaration:

My Body Is:

My Body Feels:

I Thank God For:

Today I Will Focus On:

My Exercise Goal For Today:

Today's Self-Talk:

MY NEW BODY - NIGHTLY THOUGHTS

Date:

IF I DID NOT WORK OUT TODAY
(FILL OUT THE FOLLOWING)....

How Did I Relax My Body Today?

Today I Allowed Myself:

What Changes Am I Starting To Notice?

Who Tried To Discourage Me From Working Out Today?

IF I WORKED OUT TODAY
(FILL OUT THE FOLLOWING)....

Work Out Time:

Equipment That I Used Today:

Length Of Time Spent Working Out:

While Working Out Today, I Listened To:

My Exercise Heart Rate:

Did I Have A Workout Partner/Trainer Today And If The Answer Is Yes, Who Was It?

My Heart Rate Resting:

I Motivated Myself By:

Today I Ate:

My Workout Today Consisted Of:

Today I Drank:

NIGHTLY THOUGHTS CONTINUED

Classes I Took Today (Answer If Applicable):

I Noticed:

What Parts Of My Body Feel Sore Today?

I No Longer Complain About:

What Felt Good Today?

What Tried To Discourage Me Today From Working Out?

What Did Not Feel Good Today?

I Took Advantage Of:

What Was A Challenge For Me Today?

I Am Progressing Towards:

I Am Working Through:

NEW BODY THIS MORNING

Date: Mood:

Today's Declaration:

My Body Is:

My Body Feels:

I Thank God For:

Today I Will Focus On:

My Exercise Goal For Today:

Today's Self-Talk:

MY NEW BODY - NIGHTLY THOUGHTS

Date:

IF I DID NOT WORK OUT TODAY
(FILL OUT THE FOLLOWING)....

How Did I Relax My Body Today?

Today I Allowed Myself:

What Changes Am I Starting To Notice?

Who Tried To Discourage Me From Working Out Today?

IF I WORKED OUT TODAY
(FILL OUT THE FOLLOWING)....

Work Out Time:

Equipment That I Used Today:

Length Of Time Spent Working Out:

While Working Out Today, I Listened To:

My Exercise Heart Rate:

Did I Have A Workout Partner/Trainer Today And If The Answer Is Yes, Who Was It?

My Heart Rate Resting:

I Motivated Myself By:

Today I Ate:

My Workout Today Consisted Of:

Today I Drank:

NIGHTLY THOUGHTS CONTINUED

Classes I Took Today (Answer If Applicable):

I Noticed:

What Parts Of My Body Feel Sore Today?

I No Longer Complain About:

What Felt Good Today?

What Tried To Discourage Me Today From Working Out?

What Did Not Feel Good Today?

I Took Advantage Of:

What Was A Challenge For Me Today?

I Am Progressing Towards:

I Am Working Through:

NEW BODY THIS MORNING

Date: Mood:

Today's Declaration:

My Body Is:

My Body Feels:

I Thank God For:

Today I Will Focus On:

My Exercise Goal For Today:

Today's Self-Talk:

MY NEW BODY - NIGHTLY THOUGHTS

Date:

IF I DID NOT WORK OUT TODAY
(FILL OUT THE FOLLOWING)....

How Did I Relax My Body Today?

Today I Allowed Myself:

What Changes Am I Starting To Notice?

Who Tried To Discourage Me From Working Out Today?

IF I WORKED OUT TODAY
(FILL OUT THE FOLLOWING)....

Work Out Time:

Equipment That I Used Today:

Length Of Time Spent Working Out:

While Working Out Today, I Listened To:

My Exercise Heart Rate:

Did I Have A Workout Partner/Trainer Today And If The Answer Is Yes, Who Was It?

My Heart Rate Resting:

I Motivated Myself By:

Today I Ate:

My Workout Today Consisted Of:

Today I Drank:

NIGHTLY THOUGHTS CONTINUED

Classes I Took Today (Answer If Applicable):

I Noticed:

What Parts Of My Body Feel Sore Today?

I No Longer Complain About:

What Felt Good Today?

What Tried To Discourage Me Today From Working Out?

What Did Not Feel Good Today?

I Took Advantage Of:

What Was A Challenge For Me Today?

I Am Progressing Towards:

I Am Working Through:

JUST SWEATING IT OUT.

MY WORKOUT PLAYLIST CONSISTS OF....

NEW BODY THIS MORNING

Date: Mood:

Today's Declaration:

My Body Is:

My Body Feels:

I Thank God For:

Today I Will Focus On:

My Exercise Goal For Today:

Today's Self-Talk:

MY NEW BODY - NIGHTLY THOUGHTS

Date:

IF I DID NOT WORK OUT TODAY
(FILL OUT THE FOLLOWING)....

How Did I Relax My Body Today?

Today I Allowed Myself:

What Changes Am I Starting To Notice?

Who Tried To Discourage Me From
Working Out Today?

IF I WORKED OUT TODAY
(FILL OUT THE FOLLOWING)....

Work Out Time:

Equipment That I Used Today:

Length Of Time Spent Working Out:

While Working Out Today, I Listened To:

My Exercise Heart Rate:

Did I Have A Workout Partner/Trainer Today
And If The Answer Is Yes, Who Was It?

My Heart Rate Resting:

I Motivated Myself By:

Today I Ate:

My Workout Today Consisted Of:

Today I Drank:

NIGHTLY THOUGHTS CONTINUED

Classes I Took Today (Answer If Applicable):

I Noticed:

What Parts Of My Body Feel Sore Today?

I No Longer Complain About:

What Felt Good Today?

What Tried To Discourage Me Today From Working Out?

What Did Not Feel Good Today?

I Took Advantage Of:

What Was A Challenge For Me Today?

I Am Progressing Towards:

I Am Working Through:

NEW BODY THIS MORNING

Date: Mood:

Today's Declaration:

My Body Is:

My Body Feels:

I Thank God For:

Today I Will Focus On:

My Exercise Goal For Today:

Today's Self-Talk:

MY NEW BODY - NIGHTLY THOUGHTS

Date:

IF I DID NOT WORK OUT TODAY
(FILL OUT THE FOLLOWING)....

How Did I Relax My Body Today?

Today I Allowed Myself:

What Changes Am I Starting To Notice?

Who Tried To Discourage Me From Working Out Today?

IF I WORKED OUT TODAY
(FILL OUT THE FOLLOWING)....

Work Out Time:

Equipment That I Used Today:

Length Of Time Spent Working Out:

While Working Out Today, I Listened To:

My Exercise Heart Rate:

Did I Have A Workout Partner/Trainer Today And If The Answer Is Yes, Who Was It?

My Heart Rate Resting:

I Motivated Myself By:

Today I Ate:

My Workout Today Consisted Of:

Today I Drank:

NIGHTLY THOUGHTS CONTINUED

Classes I Took Today (Answer If Applicable):

I Noticed:

What Parts Of My Body Feel Sore Today?

I No Longer Complain About:

What Felt Good Today?

What Tried To Discourage Me Today From Working Out?

What Did Not Feel Good Today?

I Took Advantage Of:

What Was A Challenge For Me Today?

I Am Progressing Towards:

I Am Working Through:

NEW BODY THIS MORNING

Date: Mood:

Today's Declaration:

My Body Is:

My Body Feels:

I Thank God For:

Today I Will Focus On:

My Exercise Goal For Today:

Today's Self-Talk:

264

MY NEW BODY - NIGHTLY THOUGHTS

Date:

IF I DID NOT WORK OUT TODAY
(FILL OUT THE FOLLOWING)....

How Did I Relax My Body Today?

What Changes Am I Starting To Notice?

Today I Allowed Myself:

Who Tried To Discourage Me From Working Out Today?

IF I WORKED OUT TODAY
(FILL OUT THE FOLLOWING)....

Work Out Time:

Length Of Time Spent Working Out:

My Exercise Heart Rate:

My Heart Rate Resting:

I Motivated Myself By:

My Workout Today Consisted Of:

Equipment That I Used Today:

While Working Out Today, I Listened To:

Did I Have A Workout Partner/Trainer Today And If The Answer Is Yes, Who Was It?

Today I Ate:

Today I Drank:

NIGHTLY THOUGHTS CONTINUED

Classes I Took Today (Answer If Applicable):

I Noticed:

What Parts Of My Body Feel Sore Today?

I No Longer Complain About:

What Felt Good Today?

What Tried To Discourage Me Today From Working Out?

What Did Not Feel Good Today?

I Took Advantage Of:

What Was A Challenge For Me Today?

I Am Progressing Towards:

I Am Working Through:

WHAT HAPPENS ONCE I REACH MY GOALS?

ACTUALLY....
I CAN.

NEW BODY THIS MORNING

Date: Mood:

Today's Declaration:

My Body Is:

My Body Feels:

I Thank God For:

Today I Will Focus On:

My Exercise Goal For Today:

Today's Self-Talk:

MY NEW BODY - NIGHTLY THOUGHTS

Date:

IF I DID NOT WORK OUT TODAY
(FILL OUT THE FOLLOWING)....

How Did I Relax My Body Today?

Today I Allowed Myself:

What Changes Am I Starting To Notice?

Who Tried To Discourage Me From
Working Out Today?

IF I WORKED OUT TODAY
(FILL OUT THE FOLLOWING)....

Work Out Time:

Equipment That I Used Today:

Length Of Time Spent Working Out:

While Working Out Today, I Listened To:

My Exercise Heart Rate:

Did I Have A Workout Partner/Trainer Today
And If The Answer Is Yes, Who Was It?

My Heart Rate Resting:

I Motivated Myself By:

Today I Ate:

My Workout Today Consisted Of:

Today I Drank:

NIGHTLY THOUGHTS CONTINUED

Classes I Took Today (Answer If Applicable):

I Noticed:

What Parts Of My Body Feel Sore Today?

I No Longer Complain About:

What Felt Good Today?

What Tried To Discourage Me Today From Working Out?

What Did Not Feel Good Today?

I Took Advantage Of:

What Was A Challenge For Me Today?

I Am Progressing Towards:

I Am Working Through:

NEW BODY THIS MORNING

Date: Mood:

Today's Declaration:

My Body Is:

My Body Feels:

I Thank God For:

Today I Will Focus On:

My Exercise Goal For Today:

Today's Self-Talk:

MY NEW BODY - NIGHTLY THOUGHTS

Date:

IF I DID NOT WORK OUT TODAY
(FILL OUT THE FOLLOWING)....

How Did I Relax My Body Today?

Today I Allowed Myself:

What Changes Am I Starting To Notice?

Who Tried To Discourage Me From Working Out Today?

IF I WORKED OUT TODAY
(FILL OUT THE FOLLOWING)....

Work Out Time:

Equipment That I Used Today:

Length Of Time Spent Working Out:

While Working Out Today, I Listened To:

My Exercise Heart Rate:

Did I Have A Workout Partner/Trainer Today And If The Answer Is Yes, Who Was It?

My Heart Rate Resting:

I Motivated Myself By:

Today I Ate:

My Workout Today Consisted Of:

Today I Drank:

NIGHTLY THOUGHTS CONTINUED

Classes I Took Today (Answer If Applicable):

I Noticed:

What Parts Of My Body Feel Sore Today?

I No Longer Complain About:

What Felt Good Today?

What Tried To Discourage Me Today From Working Out?

What Did Not Feel Good Today?

I Took Advantage Of:

What Was A Challenge For Me Today?

I Am Progressing Towards:

I Am Working Through:

NEW BODY THIS MORNING

Date: Mood:

Today's Declaration:

My Body Is:

My Body Feels:

I Thank God For:

Today I Will Focus On:

My Exercise Goal For Today:

Today's Self-Talk:

MY NEW BODY - NIGHTLY THOUGHTS

Date:

IF I DID NOT WORK OUT TODAY
(FILL OUT THE FOLLOWING)....

How Did I Relax My Body Today?

What Changes Am I Starting To Notice?

Today I Allowed Myself:

Who Tried To Discourage Me From Working Out Today?

IF I WORKED OUT TODAY
(FILL OUT THE FOLLOWING)....

Work Out Time:

Length Of Time Spent Working Out:

My Exercise Heart Rate:

My Heart Rate Resting:

I Motivated Myself By:

My Workout Today Consisted Of:

Equipment That I Used Today:

While Working Out Today, I Listened To:

Did I Have A Workout Partner/Trainer Today And If The Answer Is Yes, Who Was It?

Today I Ate:

Today I Drank:

NIGHTLY THOUGHTS CONTINUED

Classes I Took Today (Answer If Applicable):

I Noticed:

What Parts Of My Body Feel Sore Today?

I No Longer Complain About:

What Felt Good Today?

What Tried To Discourage Me Today From Working Out?

What Did Not Feel Good Today?

I Took Advantage Of:

What Was A Challenge For Me Today?

I Am Progressing Towards:

I Am Working Through:

MAKING THINGS HAPPEN.

PERSONAL THOUGHTS

NEW BODY THIS MORNING

Date: Mood:

Today's Declaration:

My Body Is:

My Body Feels:

I Thank God For:

Today I Will Focus On:

My Exercise Goal For Today:

Today's Self-Talk:

MY NEW BODY - NIGHTLY THOUGHTS

Date:

IF I DID NOT WORK OUT TODAY
(FILL OUT THE FOLLOWING)....

How Did I Relax My Body Today?

Today I Allowed Myself:

What Changes Am I Starting To Notice?

Who Tried To Discourage Me From Working Out Today?

IF I WORKED OUT TODAY
(FILL OUT THE FOLLOWING)....

Work Out Time:

Equipment That I Used Today:

Length Of Time Spent Working Out:

While Working Out Today, I Listened To:

My Exercise Heart Rate:

Did I Have A Workout Partner/Trainer Today And If The Answer Is Yes, Who Was It?

My Heart Rate Resting:

I Motivated Myself By:

Today I Ate:

My Workout Today Consisted Of:

Today I Drank:

NIGHTLY THOUGHTS CONTINUED

Classes I Took Today (Answer If Applicable):

I Noticed:

What Parts Of My Body Feel Sore Today?

I No Longer Complain About:

What Felt Good Today?

What Tried To Discourage Me Today From Working Out?

What Did Not Feel Good Today?

I Took Advantage Of:

What Was A Challenge For Me Today?

I Am Progressing Towards:

I Am Working Through:

NEW BODY THIS MORNING

Date: Mood:

Today's Declaration:

My Body Is:

My Body Feels:

I Thank God For:

Today I Will Focus On:

My Exercise Goal For Today:

Today's Self-Talk:

MY NEW BODY - NIGHTLY THOUGHTS

Date:

IF I DID NOT WORK OUT TODAY
(FILL OUT THE FOLLOWING)....

How Did I Relax My Body Today?

Today I Allowed Myself:

What Changes Am I Starting To Notice?

Who Tried To Discourage Me From Working Out Today?

IF I WORKED OUT TODAY
(FILL OUT THE FOLLOWING)....

Work Out Time:

Equipment That I Used Today:

Length Of Time Spent Working Out:

While Working Out Today, I Listened To:

My Exercise Heart Rate:

Did I Have A Workout Partner/Trainer Today And If The Answer Is Yes, Who Was It?

My Heart Rate Resting:

I Motivated Myself By:

Today I Ate:

My Workout Today Consisted Of:

Today I Drank:

NIGHTLY THOUGHTS CONTINUED

Classes I Took Today (Answer If Applicable):

I Noticed:

What Parts Of My Body Feel Sore Today?

I No Longer Complain About:

What Felt Good Today?

What Tried To Discourage Me Today From Working Out?

What Did Not Feel Good Today?

I Took Advantage Of:

What Was A Challenge For Me Today?

I Am Progressing Towards:

I Am Working Through:

NEW BODY THIS MORNING

Date: Mood:

Today's Declaration:

My Body Is:

My Body Feels:

I Thank God For:

Today I Will Focus On:

My Exercise Goal For Today:

Today's Self-Talk:

MY NEW BODY - NIGHTLY THOUGHTS

Date:

IF I DID NOT WORK OUT TODAY
(FILL OUT THE FOLLOWING)....

How Did I Relax My Body Today?

Today I Allowed Myself:

What Changes Am I Starting To Notice?

Who Tried To Discourage Me From Working Out Today?

IF I WORKED OUT TODAY
(FILL OUT THE FOLLOWING)....

Work Out Time:

Equipment That I Used Today:

Length Of Time Spent Working Out:

While Working Out Today, I Listened To:

My Exercise Heart Rate:

Did I Have A Workout Partner/Trainer Today And If The Answer Is Yes, Who Was It?

My Heart Rate Resting:

I Motivated Myself By:

Today I Ate:

My Workout Today Consisted Of:

Today I Drank:

NIGHTLY THOUGHTS CONTINUED

Classes I Took Today (Answer If Applicable):

I Noticed:

What Parts Of My Body Feel Sore Today?

I No Longer Complain About:

What Felt Good Today?

What Tried To Discourage Me Today From Working Out?

What Did Not Feel Good Today?

I Took Advantage Of:

What Was A Challenge For Me Today?

I Am Progressing Towards:

I Am Working Through:

FIVE THINGS THAT I AM PROUD OF....

1.

2.

3.

4.

5.

WHATEVER I TELL MY MIND, MY BODY WILL FOLLOW.

NEW BODY THIS MORNING

Date: Mood:

Today's Declaration:

My Body Is:

My Body Feels:

I Thank God For:

Today I Will Focus On:

My Exercise Goal For Today:

Today's Self-Talk:

MY NEW BODY - NIGHTLY THOUGHTS

Date:

IF I DID NOT WORK OUT TODAY
(FILL OUT THE FOLLOWING)....

How Did I Relax My Body Today?

Today I Allowed Myself:

What Changes Am I Starting To Notice?

Who Tried To Discourage Me From Working Out Today?

IF I WORKED OUT TODAY
(FILL OUT THE FOLLOWING)....

Work Out Time:

Equipment That I Used Today:

Length Of Time Spent Working Out:

While Working Out Today, I Listened To:

My Exercise Heart Rate:

Did I Have A Workout Partner/Trainer Today And If The Answer Is Yes, Who Was It?

My Heart Rate Resting:

I Motivated Myself By:

Today I Ate:

My Workout Today Consisted Of:

Today I Drank:

NIGHTLY THOUGHTS CONTINUED

Classes I Took Today (Answer If Applicable):

I Noticed:

What Parts Of My Body Feel Sore Today?

I No Longer Complain About:

What Felt Good Today?

What Tried To Discourage Me Today From Working Out?

What Did Not Feel Good Today?

I Took Advantage Of:

What Was A Challenge For Me Today?

I Am Progressing Towards:

I Am Working Through:

NEW BODY THIS MORNING

Date: Mood:

Today's Declaration:

My Body Is:

My Body Feels:

I Thank God For:

Today I Will Focus On:

My Exercise Goal For Today:

Today's Self-Talk:

MY NEW BODY - NIGHTLY THOUGHTS

Date:

IF I DID NOT WORK OUT TODAY
(FILL OUT THE FOLLOWING)....

How Did I Relax My Body Today?

Today I Allowed Myself:

What Changes Am I Starting To Notice?

Who Tried To Discourage Me From Working Out Today?

IF I WORKED OUT TODAY
(FILL OUT THE FOLLOWING)....

Work Out Time:

Equipment That I Used Today:

Length Of Time Spent Working Out:

While Working Out Today, I Listened To:

My Exercise Heart Rate:

Did I Have A Workout Partner/Trainer Today And If The Answer Is Yes, Who Was It?

My Heart Rate Resting:

I Motivated Myself By:

Today I Ate:

My Workout Today Consisted Of:

Today I Drank:

NIGHTLY THOUGHTS CONTINUED

Classes I Took Today (Answer If Applicable):

I Noticed:

What Parts Of My Body Feel Sore Today?

I No Longer Complain About:

What Felt Good Today?

What Tried To Discourage Me Today From Working Out?

What Did Not Feel Good Today?

I Took Advantage Of:

What Was A Challenge For Me Today?

I Am Progressing Towards:

I Am Working Through:

NEW BODY THIS MORNING

Date:

Mood:

Today's Declaration:

My Body Is:

My Body Feels:

I Thank God For:

Today I Will Focus On:

My Exercise Goal For Today:

Today's Self-Talk:

MY NEW BODY - NIGHTLY THOUGHTS

Date:

IF I DID NOT WORK OUT TODAY
(FILL OUT THE FOLLOWING)....

How Did I Relax My Body Today?

Today I Allowed Myself:

What Changes Am I Starting To Notice?

Who Tried To Discourage Me From Working Out Today?

IF I WORKED OUT TODAY
(FILL OUT THE FOLLOWING)....

Work Out Time:

Equipment That I Used Today:

Length Of Time Spent Working Out:

While Working Out Today, I Listened To:

My Exercise Heart Rate:

Did I Have A Workout Partner/Trainer Today And If The Answer Is Yes, Who Was It?

My Heart Rate Resting:

I Motivated Myself By:

Today I Ate:

My Workout Today Consisted Of:

Today I Drank:

NIGHTLY THOUGHTS CONTINUED

Classes I Took Today (Answer If Applicable):

I Noticed:

What Parts Of My Body Feel Sore Today?

I No Longer Complain About:

What Felt Good Today?

What Tried To Discourage Me Today From Working Out?

What Did Not Feel Good Today?

I Took Advantage Of:

What Was A Challenge For Me Today?

I Am Progressing Towards:

I Am Working Through:

SQUAT LIFE.

PERSONAL THOUGHTS

NEW BODY THIS MORNING

Date: Mood:

Today's Declaration:

My Body Is:

My Body Feels:

I Thank God For:

Today I Will Focus On:

My Exercise Goal For Today:

Today's Self-Talk:

302

MY NEW BODY - NIGHTLY THOUGHTS

Date:

IF I DID NOT WORK OUT TODAY
(FILL OUT THE FOLLOWING)....

How Did I Relax My Body Today?

Today I Allowed Myself:

What Changes Am I Starting To Notice?

Who Tried To Discourage Me From
Working Out Today?

IF I WORKED OUT TODAY
(FILL OUT THE FOLLOWING)....

Work Out Time:

Equipment That I Used Today:

Length Of Time Spent Working Out:

While Working Out Today, I Listened To:

My Exercise Heart Rate:

Did I Have A Workout Partner/Trainer Today
And If The Answer Is Yes, Who Was It?

My Heart Rate Resting:

I Motivated Myself By:

Today I Ate:

My Workout Today Consisted Of:

Today I Drank:

NIGHTLY THOUGHTS CONTINUED

Classes I Took Today (Answer If Applicable):

I Noticed:

What Parts Of My Body Feel Sore Today?

I No Longer Complain About:

What Felt Good Today?

What Tried To Discourage Me Today From Working Out?

What Did Not Feel Good Today?

I Took Advantage Of:

What Was A Challenge For Me Today?

I Am Progressing Towards:

I Am Working Through:

NEW BODY THIS MORNING

Date: Mood:

Today's Declaration:

My Body Is:

My Body Feels:

I Thank God For:

Today I Will Focus On:

My Exercise Goal For Today:

Today's Self-Talk:

MY NEW BODY - NIGHTLY THOUGHTS

Date:

IF I DID NOT WORK OUT TODAY
(FILL OUT THE FOLLOWING)....

How Did I Relax My Body Today?

Today I Allowed Myself:

What Changes Am I Starting To Notice?

Who Tried To Discourage Me From Working Out Today?

IF I WORKED OUT TODAY
(FILL OUT THE FOLLOWING)....

Work Out Time:

Equipment That I Used Today:

Length Of Time Spent Working Out:

While Working Out Today, I Listened To:

My Exercise Heart Rate:

Did I Have A Workout Partner/Trainer Today And If The Answer Is Yes, Who Was It?

My Heart Rate Resting:

I Motivated Myself By:

Today I Ate:

My Workout Today Consisted Of:

Today I Drank:

NIGHTLY THOUGHTS CONTINUED

Classes I Took Today (Answer If Applicable):

I Noticed:

What Parts Of My Body Feel Sore Today?

I No Longer Complain About:

What Felt Good Today?

What Tried To Discourage Me Today From Working Out?

What Did Not Feel Good Today?

I Took Advantage Of:

What Was A Challenge For Me Today?

I Am Progressing Towards:

I Am Working Through:

NEW BODY THIS MORNING

Date: Mood:

Today's Declaration:

My Body Is:

My Body Feels:

I Thank God For:

Today I Will Focus On:

My Exercise Goal For Today:

Today's Self-Talk:

MY NEW BODY - NIGHTLY THOUGHTS

Date:

IF I DID NOT WORK OUT TODAY
(FILL OUT THE FOLLOWING)....

How Did I Relax My Body Today?

Today I Allowed Myself:

What Changes Am I Starting To Notice?

Who Tried To Discourage Me From
Working Out Today?

IF I WORKED OUT TODAY
(FILL OUT THE FOLLOWING)....

Work Out Time:

Equipment That I Used Today:

Length Of Time Spent Working Out:

While Working Out Today, I Listened To:

My Exercise Heart Rate:

Did I Have A Workout Partner/Trainer Today
And If The Answer Is Yes, Who Was It?

My Heart Rate Resting:

I Motivated Myself By:

Today I Ate:

My Workout Today Consisted Of:

Today I Drank:

NIGHTLY THOUGHTS CONTINUED

Classes I Took Today (Answer If Applicable):

I Noticed:

What Parts Of My Body Feel Sore Today?

I No Longer Complain About:

What Felt Good Today?

What Tried To Discourage Me Today From Working Out?

What Did Not Feel Good Today?

I Took Advantage Of:

What Was A Challenge For Me Today?

I Am Progressing Towards:

I Am Working Through:

I AM BECOMING....

MOVE.
MOVE.
MOVE.

NEW BODY THIS MORNING

Date: Mood:

Today's Declaration:

My Body Is:

My Body Feels:

I Thank God For:

Today I Will Focus On:

My Exercise Goal For Today:

Today's Self-Talk:

MY NEW BODY - NIGHTLY THOUGHTS

Date:

IF I DID NOT WORK OUT TODAY
(FILL OUT THE FOLLOWING)....

How Did I Relax My Body Today?

Today I Allowed Myself:

What Changes Am I Starting To Notice?

Who Tried To Discourage Me From Working Out Today?

IF I WORKED OUT TODAY
(FILL OUT THE FOLLOWING)....

Work Out Time:

Equipment That I Used Today:

Length Of Time Spent Working Out:

While Working Out Today, I Listened To:

My Exercise Heart Rate:

Did I Have A Workout Partner/Trainer Today And If The Answer Is Yes, Who Was It?

My Heart Rate Resting:

I Motivated Myself By:

Today I Ate:

My Workout Today Consisted Of:

Today I Drank:

NIGHTLY THOUGHTS CONTINUED

Classes I Took Today (Answer If Applicable):

I Noticed:

What Parts Of My Body Feel Sore Today?

I No Longer Complain About:

What Felt Good Today?

What Tried To Discourage Me Today From Working Out?

What Did Not Feel Good Today?

I Took Advantage Of:

What Was A Challenge For Me Today?

I Am Progressing Towards:

I Am Working Through:

NEW BODY THIS MORNING

Date: Mood:

Today's Declaration:

My Body Is:

My Body Feels:

I Thank God For:

Today I Will Focus On:

My Exercise Goal For Today:

Today's Self-Talk:

MY NEW BODY - NIGHTLY THOUGHTS

Date:

IF I DID NOT WORK OUT TODAY
(FILL OUT THE FOLLOWING)....

How Did I Relax My Body Today?

Today I Allowed Myself:

What Changes Am I Starting To Notice?

Who Tried To Discourage Me From Working Out Today?

IF I WORKED OUT TODAY
(FILL OUT THE FOLLOWING)....

Work Out Time:

Equipment That I Used Today:

Length Of Time Spent Working Out:

While Working Out Today, I Listened To:

My Exercise Heart Rate:

Did I Have A Workout Partner/Trainer Today And If The Answer Is Yes, Who Was It?

My Heart Rate Resting:

I Motivated Myself By:

Today I Ate:

My Workout Today Consisted Of:

Today I Drank:

NIGHTLY THOUGHTS CONTINUED

Classes I Took Today (Answer If Applicable):

I Noticed:

What Parts Of My Body Feel Sore Today?

I No Longer Complain About:

What Felt Good Today?

What Tried To Discourage Me Today From Working Out?

What Did Not Feel Good Today?

I Took Advantage Of:

What Was A Challenge For Me Today?

I Am Progressing Towards:

I Am Working Through:

NEW BODY THIS MORNING

Date: Mood:

Today's Declaration:

My Body Is:

My Body Feels:

I Thank God For:

Today I Will Focus On:

My Exercise Goal For Today:

Today's Self-Talk:

MY NEW BODY - NIGHTLY THOUGHTS

Date:

IF I DID NOT WORK OUT TODAY
(FILL OUT THE FOLLOWING)....

How Did I Relax My Body Today?

Today I Allowed Myself:

What Changes Am I Starting To Notice?

Who Tried To Discourage Me From Working Out Today?

IF I WORKED OUT TODAY
(FILL OUT THE FOLLOWING)....

Work Out Time:

Equipment That I Used Today:

Length Of Time Spent Working Out:

While Working Out Today, I Listened To:

My Exercise Heart Rate:

Did I Have A Workout Partner/Trainer Today And If The Answer Is Yes, Who Was It?

My Heart Rate Resting:

I Motivated Myself By:

Today I Ate:

My Workout Today Consisted Of:

Today I Drank:

NIGHTLY THOUGHTS CONTINUED

Classes I Took Today (Answer If Applicable):

I Noticed:

What Parts Of My Body Feel Sore Today?

I No Longer Complain About:

What Felt Good Today?

What Tried To Discourage Me Today From Working Out?

What Did Not Feel Good Today?

I Took Advantage Of:

What Was A Challenge For Me Today?

I Am Progressing Towards:

I Am Working Through:

INVESTING IN MY HEALTH.

PERSONAL THOUGHTS

NEW BODY THIS MORNING

Date: Mood:

Today's Declaration:

My Body Is:

My Body Feels:

I Thank God For:

Today I Will Focus On:

My Exercise Goal For Today:

Today's Self-Talk:

324

MY NEW BODY - NIGHTLY THOUGHTS

Date:

IF I DID NOT WORK OUT TODAY
(FILL OUT THE FOLLOWING)....

How Did I Relax My Body Today?

Today I Allowed Myself:

What Changes Am I Starting To Notice?

Who Tried To Discourage Me From Working Out Today?

IF I WORKED OUT TODAY
(FILL OUT THE FOLLOWING)....

Work Out Time:

Equipment That I Used Today:

Length Of Time Spent Working Out:

While Working Out Today, I Listened To:

My Exercise Heart Rate:

Did I Have A Workout Partner/Trainer Today And If The Answer Is Yes, Who Was It?

My Heart Rate Resting:

I Motivated Myself By:

Today I Ate:

My Workout Today Consisted Of:

Today I Drank:

NIGHTLY THOUGHTS CONTINUED

Classes I Took Today (Answer If Applicable):

I Noticed:

What Parts Of My Body Feel Sore Today?

I No Longer Complain About:

What Felt Good Today?

What Tried To Discourage Me Today From Working Out?

What Did Not Feel Good Today?

I Took Advantage Of:

What Was A Challenge For Me Today?

I Am Progressing Towards:

I Am Working Through:

NEW BODY THIS MORNING

Date: Mood:

Today's Declaration:

My Body Is:

My Body Feels:

I Thank God For:

Today I Will Focus On:

My Exercise Goal For Today:

Today's Self-Talk:

MY NEW BODY - NIGHTLY THOUGHTS

Date:

IF I DID NOT WORK OUT TODAY
(FILL OUT THE FOLLOWING)....

How Did I Relax My Body Today?

Today I Allowed Myself:

What Changes Am I Starting To Notice?

Who Tried To Discourage Me From Working Out Today?

IF I WORKED OUT TODAY
(FILL OUT THE FOLLOWING)....

Work Out Time:

Equipment That I Used Today:

Length Of Time Spent Working Out:

While Working Out Today, I Listened To:

My Exercise Heart Rate:

Did I Have A Workout Partner/Trainer Today And If The Answer Is Yes, Who Was It?

My Heart Rate Resting:

I Motivated Myself By:

Today I Ate:

My Workout Today Consisted Of:

Today I Drank:

NIGHTLY THOUGHTS CONTINUED

Classes I Took Today (Answer If Applicable):

I Noticed:

What Parts Of My Body Feel Sore Today?

I No Longer Complain About:

What Felt Good Today?

What Tried To Discourage Me Today From Working Out?

What Did Not Feel Good Today?

I Took Advantage Of:

What Was A Challenge For Me Today?

I Am Progressing Towards:

I Am Working Through:

NEW BODY THIS MORNING

Date: Mood:

Today's Declaration:

My Body Is:

My Body Feels:

I Thank God For:

Today I Will Focus On:

My Exercise Goal For Today:

Today's Self-Talk:

MY NEW BODY - NIGHTLY THOUGHTS

Date:

IF I DID NOT WORK OUT TODAY
(FILL OUT THE FOLLOWING)....

How Did I Relax My Body Today?

Today I Allowed Myself:

What Changes Am I Starting To Notice?

Who Tried To Discourage Me From Working Out Today?

IF I WORKED OUT TODAY
(FILL OUT THE FOLLOWING)....

Work Out Time:

Equipment That I Used Today:

Length Of Time Spent Working Out:

While Working Out Today, I Listened To:

My Exercise Heart Rate:

Did I Have A Workout Partner/Trainer Today And If The Answer Is Yes, Who Was It?

My Heart Rate Resting:

I Motivated Myself By:

Today I Ate:

My Workout Today Consisted Of:

Today I Drank:

NIGHTLY THOUGHTS CONTINUED

Classes I Took Today (Answer If Applicable):

I Noticed:

What Parts Of My Body Feel Sore Today?

I No Longer Complain About:

What Felt Good Today?

What Tried To Discourage Me Today From Working Out?

What Did Not Feel Good Today?

I Took Advantage Of:

What Was A Challenge For Me Today?

I Am Progressing Towards:

I Am Working Through:

WHAT FIVE HEALTHY CHOICES AM I MAKING FOR MYSELF?

1.

2.

3.

4.

5.

I AM ONLY GETTING BETTER.

NEW BODY THIS MORNING

Date: Mood:

Today's Declaration:

My Body Is:

My Body Feels:

I Thank God For:

Today I Will Focus On:

My Exercise Goal For Today:

Today's Self-Talk:

MY NEW BODY - NIGHTLY THOUGHTS

Date:

IF I DID NOT WORK OUT TODAY
(FILL OUT THE FOLLOWING)....

How Did I Relax My Body Today?

Today I Allowed Myself:

What Changes Am I Starting To Notice?

Who Tried To Discourage Me From Working Out Today?

IF I WORKED OUT TODAY
(FILL OUT THE FOLLOWING)....

Work Out Time:

Equipment That I Used Today:

Length Of Time Spent Working Out:

While Working Out Today, I Listened To:

My Exercise Heart Rate:

Did I Have A Workout Partner/Trainer Today And If The Answer Is Yes, Who Was It?

My Heart Rate Resting:

I Motivated Myself By:

Today I Ate:

My Workout Today Consisted Of:

Today I Drank:

NIGHTLY THOUGHTS CONTINUED

Classes I Took Today (Answer If Applicable):

I Noticed:

What Parts Of My Body Feel Sore Today?

I No Longer Complain About:

What Felt Good Today?

What Tried To Discourage Me Today From Working Out?

What Did Not Feel Good Today?

I Took Advantage Of:

What Was A Challenge For Me Today?

I Am Progressing Towards:

I Am Working Through:

NEW BODY THIS MORNING

Date: Mood:

Today's Declaration:

My Body Is:

My Body Feels:

I Thank God For:

Today I Will Focus On:

My Exercise Goal For Today:

Today's Self-Talk:

MY NEW BODY - NIGHTLY THOUGHTS

Date:

IF I DID NOT WORK OUT TODAY
(FILL OUT THE FOLLOWING)....

How Did I Relax My Body Today?

Today I Allowed Myself:

What Changes Am I Starting To Notice?

Who Tried To Discourage Me From
Working Out Today?

IF I WORKED OUT TODAY
(FILL OUT THE FOLLOWING)....

Work Out Time:

Equipment That I Used Today:

Length Of Time Spent Working Out:

While Working Out Today, I Listened To:

My Exercise Heart Rate:

Did I Have A Workout Partner/Trainer Today
And If The Answer Is Yes, Who Was It?

My Heart Rate Resting:

I Motivated Myself By:

Today I Ate:

My Workout Today Consisted Of:

Today I Drank:

NIGHTLY THOUGHTS CONTINUED

Classes I Took Today (Answer If Applicable):

I Noticed:

What Parts Of My Body Feel Sore Today?

I No Longer Complain About:

What Felt Good Today?

What Tried To Discourage Me Today From Working Out?

What Did Not Feel Good Today?

I Took Advantage Of:

What Was A Challenge For Me Today?

I Am Progressing Towards:

I Am Working Through:

NEW BODY THIS MORNING

Date: Mood:

Today's Declaration:

My Body Is:

My Body Feels:

I Thank God For:

Today I Will Focus On:

My Exercise Goal For Today:

Today's Self-Talk:

MY NEW BODY - NIGHTLY THOUGHTS

Date:

IF I DID NOT WORK OUT TODAY
(FILL OUT THE FOLLOWING)....

How Did I Relax My Body Today?

Today I Allowed Myself:

What Changes Am I Starting To Notice?

Who Tried To Discourage Me From Working Out Today?

IF I WORKED OUT TODAY
(FILL OUT THE FOLLOWING)....

Work Out Time:

Equipment That I Used Today:

Length Of Time Spent Working Out:

While Working Out Today, I Listened To:

My Exercise Heart Rate:

Did I Have A Workout Partner/Trainer Today And If The Answer Is Yes, Who Was It?

My Heart Rate Resting:

I Motivated Myself By:

Today I Ate:

My Workout Today Consisted Of:

Today I Drank:

NIGHTLY THOUGHTS CONTINUED

Classes I Took Today (Answer If Applicable):

I Noticed:

What Parts Of My Body Feel Sore Today?

I No Longer Complain About:

What Felt Good Today?

What Tried To Discourage Me Today From Working Out?

What Did Not Feel Good Today?

I Took Advantage Of:

What Was A Challenge For Me Today?

I Am Progressing Towards:

I Am Working Through:

I LOST ALL MY EXCUSES ONLY TO FIND RESULTS.

I WAS CHALLENGED. THEN I WON.

NEW BODY THIS MORNING

Date: Mood:

Today's Declaration:

My Body Is:

My Body Feels:

I Thank God For:

Today I Will Focus On:

My Exercise Goal For Today:

Today's Self-Talk:

MY NEW BODY - NIGHTLY THOUGHTS

Date:

IF I DID NOT WORK OUT TODAY
(FILL OUT THE FOLLOWING)....

How Did I Relax My Body Today?

Today I Allowed Myself:

What Changes Am I Starting To Notice?

Who Tried To Discourage Me From
Working Out Today?

IF I WORKED OUT TODAY
(FILL OUT THE FOLLOWING)....

Work Out Time:

Equipment That I Used Today:

Length Of Time Spent Working Out:

While Working Out Today, I Listened To:

My Exercise Heart Rate:

Did I Have A Workout Partner/Trainer Today
And If The Answer Is Yes, Who Was It?

My Heart Rate Resting:

I Motivated Myself By:

Today I Ate:

My Workout Today Consisted Of:

Today I Drank:

NIGHTLY THOUGHTS CONTINUED

Classes I Took Today (Answer If Applicable):

What Parts Of My Body Feel Sore Today?

What Felt Good Today?

What Did Not Feel Good Today?

What Was A Challenge For Me Today?

I Am Working Through:

I Noticed:

I No Longer Complain About:

What Tried To Discourage Me Today From Working Out?

I Took Advantage Of:

I Am Progressing Towards:

NEW BODY THIS MORNING

Date: Mood:

Today's Declaration:

My Body Is:

My Body Feels:

I Thank God For:

Today I Will Focus On:

My Exercise Goal For Today:

Today's Self-Talk:

MY NEW BODY - NIGHTLY THOUGHTS

Date:

IF I DID NOT WORK OUT TODAY
(FILL OUT THE FOLLOWING)....

How Did I Relax My Body Today?

Today I Allowed Myself:

What Changes Am I Starting To Notice?

Who Tried To Discourage Me From Working Out Today?

IF I WORKED OUT TODAY
(FILL OUT THE FOLLOWING)....

Work Out Time:

Equipment That I Used Today:

Length Of Time Spent Working Out:

While Working Out Today, I Listened To:

My Exercise Heart Rate:

Did I Have A Workout Partner/Trainer Today And If The Answer Is Yes, Who Was It?

My Heart Rate Resting:

I Motivated Myself By:

Today I Ate:

My Workout Today Consisted Of:

Today I Drank:

NIGHTLY THOUGHTS CONTINUED

Classes I Took Today (Answer If Applicable):

I Noticed:

What Parts Of My Body Feel Sore Today?

I No Longer Complain About:

What Felt Good Today?

What Tried To Discourage Me Today From Working Out?

What Did Not Feel Good Today?

I Took Advantage Of:

What Was A Challenge For Me Today?

I Am Progressing Towards:

I Am Working Through:

NEW BODY THIS MORNING

Date: Mood:

Today's Declaration:

My Body Is:

My Body Feels:

I Thank God For:

Today I Will Focus On:

My Exercise Goal For Today:

Today's Self-Talk:

MY NEW BODY – NIGHTLY THOUGHTS

Date:

IF I DID NOT WORK OUT TODAY
(FILL OUT THE FOLLOWING)....

How Did I Relax My Body Today?

What Changes Am I Starting To Notice?

Today I Allowed Myself:

Who Tried To Discourage Me From
Working Out Today?

IF I WORKED OUT TODAY
(FILL OUT THE FOLLOWING)....

Work Out Time:

Length Of Time Spent Working Out:

My Exercise Heart Rate:

My Heart Rate Resting:

I Motivated Myself By:

My Workout Today Consisted Of:

Equipment That I Used Today:

While Working Out Today, I Listened To:

Did I Have A Workout Partner/Trainer Today
And If The Answer Is Yes, Who Was It?

Today I Ate:

Today I Drank:

NIGHTLY THOUGHTS CONTINUED

Classes I Took Today (Answer If Applicable):

I Noticed:

What Parts Of My Body Feel Sore Today?

I No Longer Complain About:

What Felt Good Today?

What Tried To Discourage Me Today From Working Out?

What Did Not Feel Good Today?

I Took Advantage Of:

What Was A Challenge For Me Today?

I Am Progressing Towards:

I Am Working Through:

I WORKOUT BECAUSE I CAN.

JUST RESPECTING MY BODY.

NEW BODY THIS MORNING

Date: Mood:

Today's Declaration:

My Body Is:

My Body Feels:

I Thank God For:

Today I Will Focus On:

My Exercise Goal For Today:

Today's Self-Talk:

MY NEW BODY - NIGHTLY THOUGHTS

Date:

IF I DID NOT WORK OUT TODAY
(FILL OUT THE FOLLOWING)....

How Did I Relax My Body Today?

Today I Allowed Myself:

What Changes Am I Starting To Notice?

Who Tried To Discourage Me From Working Out Today?

IF I WORKED OUT TODAY
(FILL OUT THE FOLLOWING)....

Work Out Time:

Equipment That I Used Today:

Length Of Time Spent Working Out:

While Working Out Today, I Listened To:

My Exercise Heart Rate:

Did I Have A Workout Partner/Trainer Today And If The Answer Is Yes, Who Was It?

My Heart Rate Resting:

I Motivated Myself By:

Today I Ate:

My Workout Today Consisted Of:

Today I Drank:

NIGHTLY THOUGHTS CONTINUED

Classes I Took Today (Answer If Applicable):

I Noticed:

What Parts Of My Body Feel Sore Today?

I No Longer Complain About:

What Felt Good Today?

What Tried To Discourage Me Today From Working Out?

What Did Not Feel Good Today?

I Took Advantage Of:

What Was A Challenge For Me Today?

I Am Progressing Towards:

I Am Working Through:

NEW BODY THIS MORNING

Date: Mood:

Today's Declaration:

My Body Is:

My Body Feels:

I Thank God For:

Today I Will Focus On:

My Exercise Goal For Today:

Today's Self-Talk:

MY NEW BODY - NIGHTLY THOUGHTS

Date:

IF I DID NOT WORK OUT TODAY
(FILL OUT THE FOLLOWING)....

How Did I Relax My Body Today?

Today I Allowed Myself:

What Changes Am I Starting To Notice?

Who Tried To Discourage Me From
Working Out Today?

IF I WORKED OUT TODAY
(FILL OUT THE FOLLOWING)....

Work Out Time:

Equipment That I Used Today:

Length Of Time Spent Working Out:

While Working Out Today, I Listened To:

My Exercise Heart Rate:

Did I Have A Workout Partner/Trainer Today
And If The Answer Is Yes, Who Was It?

My Heart Rate Resting:

I Motivated Myself By:

Today I Ate:

My Workout Today Consisted Of:

Today I Drank:

NIGHTLY THOUGHTS CONTINUED

Classes I Took Today (Answer If Applicable):

I Noticed:

What Parts Of My Body Feel Sore Today?

I No Longer Complain About:

What Felt Good Today?

What Tried To Discourage Me Today From Working Out?

What Did Not Feel Good Today?

I Took Advantage Of:

What Was A Challenge For Me Today?

I Am Progressing Towards:

I Am Working Through:

NEW BODY THIS MORNING

Date: Mood:

Today's Declaration:

My Body Is:

My Body Feels:

I Thank God For:

Today I Will Focus On:

My Exercise Goal For Today:

Today's Self-Talk:

MY NEW BODY - NIGHTLY THOUGHTS

Date:

IF I DID NOT WORK OUT TODAY
(FILL OUT THE FOLLOWING)....

How Did I Relax My Body Today?

Today I Allowed Myself:

What Changes Am I Starting To Notice?

Who Tried To Discourage Me From Working Out Today?

IF I WORKED OUT TODAY
(FILL OUT THE FOLLOWING)....

Work Out Time:

Equipment That I Used Today:

Length Of Time Spent Working Out:

While Working Out Today, I Listened To:

My Exercise Heart Rate:

Did I Have A Workout Partner/Trainer Today And If The Answer Is Yes, Who Was It?

My Heart Rate Resting:

I Motivated Myself By:

Today I Ate:

My Workout Today Consisted Of:

Today I Drank:

NIGHTLY THOUGHTS CONTINUED

Classes I Took Today (Answer If Applicable):

What Parts Of My Body Feel Sore Today?

What Felt Good Today?

What Did Not Feel Good Today?

What Was A Challenge For Me Today?

I Am Working Through:

I Noticed:

I No Longer Complain About:

What Tried To Discourage Me Today From Working Out?

I Took Advantage Of:

I Am Progressing Towards:

GET OUT OF MY WAY. I AM JUST GOING TO GO HARDER.

I AM JUST GETTING STRONGER.

NEW BODY THIS MORNING

Date: Mood:

Today's Declaration:

My Body Is:

My Body Feels:

I Thank God For:

Today I Will Focus On:

My Exercise Goal For Today:

Today's Self-Talk:

MY NEW BODY - NIGHTLY THOUGHTS

Date:

IF I DID NOT WORK OUT TODAY
(FILL OUT THE FOLLOWING)....

How Did I Relax My Body Today?

Today I Allowed Myself:

What Changes Am I Starting To Notice?

Who Tried To Discourage Me From Working Out Today?

IF I WORKED OUT TODAY
(FILL OUT THE FOLLOWING)....

Work Out Time:

Equipment That I Used Today:

Length Of Time Spent Working Out:

While Working Out Today, I Listened To:

My Exercise Heart Rate:

Did I Have A Workout Partner/Trainer Today And If The Answer Is Yes, Who Was It?

My Heart Rate Resting:

I Motivated Myself By:

Today I Ate:

My Workout Today Consisted Of:

Today I Drank:

NIGHTLY THOUGHTS CONTINUED

Classes I Took Today (Answer If Applicable):

I Noticed:

What Parts Of My Body Feel Sore Today?

I No Longer Complain About:

What Felt Good Today?

What Tried To Discourage Me Today From Working Out?

What Did Not Feel Good Today?

I Took Advantage Of:

What Was A Challenge For Me Today?

I Am Progressing Towards:

I Am Working Through:

NEW BODY THIS MORNING

Date: Mood:

Today's Declaration:

My Body Is:

My Body Feels:

I Thank God For:

Today I Will Focus On:

My Exercise Goal For Today:

Today's Self-Talk:

MY NEW BODY - NIGHTLY THOUGHTS

Date:

IF I DID NOT WORK OUT TODAY
(FILL OUT THE FOLLOWING)....

How Did I Relax My Body Today?

Today I Allowed Myself:

What Changes Am I Starting To Notice?

Who Tried To Discourage Me From
Working Out Today?

IF I WORKED OUT TODAY
(FILL OUT THE FOLLOWING)....

Work Out Time:

Equipment That I Used Today:

Length Of Time Spent Working Out:

While Working Out Today, I Listened To:

My Exercise Heart Rate:

Did I Have A Workout Partner/Trainer Today
And If The Answer Is Yes, Who Was It?

My Heart Rate Resting:

I Motivated Myself By:

Today I Ate:

My Workout Today Consisted Of:

Today I Drank:

NIGHTLY THOUGHTS CONTINUED

Classes I Took Today (Answer If Applicable):

What Parts Of My Body Feel Sore Today?

What Felt Good Today?

What Did Not Feel Good Today?

What Was A Challenge For Me Today?

I Am Working Through:

I Noticed:

I No Longer Complain About:

What Tried To Discourage Me Today From Working Out?

I Took Advantage Of:

I Am Progressing Towards:

NEW BODY THIS MORNING

Date: Mood:

Today's Declaration:

My Body Is:

My Body Feels:

I Thank God For:

Today I Will Focus On:

My Exercise Goal For Today:

Today's Self-Talk:

MY NEW BODY - NIGHTLY THOUGHTS

Date:

IF I DID NOT WORK OUT TODAY
(FILL OUT THE FOLLOWING)....

How Did I Relax My Body Today?

Today I Allowed Myself:

What Changes Am I Starting To Notice?

Who Tried To Discourage Me From Working Out Today?

IF I WORKED OUT TODAY
(FILL OUT THE FOLLOWING)....

Work Out Time:

Equipment That I Used Today:

Length Of Time Spent Working Out:

While Working Out Today, I Listened To:

My Exercise Heart Rate:

Did I Have A Workout Partner/Trainer Today And If The Answer Is Yes, Who Was It?

My Heart Rate Resting:

I Motivated Myself By:

Today I Ate:

My Workout Today Consisted Of:

Today I Drank:

NIGHTLY THOUGHTS CONTINUED

Classes I Took Today (Answer If Applicable):

I Noticed:

What Parts Of My Body Feel Sore Today?

I No Longer Complain About:

What Felt Good Today?

What Tried To Discourage Me Today From Working Out?

What Did Not Feel Good Today?

I Took Advantage Of:

What Was A Challenge For Me Today?

I Am Progressing Towards:

I Am Working Through:

I AM EVERYTHING I NEED.

DOING THIS WITH A PURPOSE.

NEW BODY THIS MORNING

Date: Mood:

Today's Declaration:

My Body Is:

My Body Feels:

I Thank God For:

Today I Will Focus On:

My Exercise Goal For Today:

Today's Self-Talk:

MY NEW BODY - NIGHTLY THOUGHTS

Date:

IF I DID NOT WORK OUT TODAY
(FILL OUT THE FOLLOWING)....

How Did I Relax My Body Today?

Today I Allowed Myself:

What Changes Am I Starting To Notice?

Who Tried To Discourage Me From Working Out Today?

IF I WORKED OUT TODAY
(FILL OUT THE FOLLOWING)....

Work Out Time:

Equipment That I Used Today:

Length Of Time Spent Working Out:

While Working Out Today, I Listened To:

My Exercise Heart Rate:

Did I Have A Workout Partner/Trainer Today And If The Answer Is Yes, Who Was It?

My Heart Rate Resting:

I Motivated Myself By:

Today I Ate:

My Workout Today Consisted Of:

Today I Drank:

NIGHTLY THOUGHTS CONTINUED

Classes I Took Today (Answer If Applicable):

I Noticed:

What Parts Of My Body Feel Sore Today?

I No Longer Complain About:

What Felt Good Today?

What Tried To Discourage Me Today From Working Out?

What Did Not Feel Good Today?

I Took Advantage Of:

What Was A Challenge For Me Today?

I Am Progressing Towards:

I Am Working Through:

NEW BODY THIS MORNING

Date: Mood:

Today's Declaration:

My Body Is:

My Body Feels:

I Thank God For:

Today I Will Focus On:

My Exercise Goal For Today:

Today's Self-Talk:

MY NEW BODY - NIGHTLY THOUGHTS

Date:

IF I DID NOT WORK OUT TODAY
(FILL OUT THE FOLLOWING)....

How Did I Relax My Body Today?

Today I Allowed Myself:

What Changes Am I Starting To Notice?

Who Tried To Discourage Me From
Working Out Today?

IF I WORKED OUT TODAY
(FILL OUT THE FOLLOWING)....

Work Out Time:

Equipment That I Used Today:

Length Of Time Spent Working Out:

While Working Out Today, I Listened To:

My Exercise Heart Rate:

Did I Have A Workout Partner/Trainer Today
And If The Answer Is Yes, Who Was It?

My Heart Rate Resting:

I Motivated Myself By:

Today I Ate:

My Workout Today Consisted Of:

Today I Drank:

NIGHTLY THOUGHTS CONTINUED

Classes I Took Today (Answer If Applicable):

I Noticed:

What Parts Of My Body Feel Sore Today?

I No Longer Complain About:

What Felt Good Today?

What Tried To Discourage Me Today From Working Out?

What Did Not Feel Good Today?

I Took Advantage Of:

What Was A Challenge For Me Today?

I Am Progressing Towards:

I Am Working Through:

I AM
POWERFUL.

PERSONAL THOUGHTS

NEW BODY THIS MORNING

Date: Mood:

Today's Declaration:

My Body Is:

My Body Feels:

I Thank God For:

Today I Will Focus On:

My Exercise Goal For Today:

Today's Self-Talk:

MY NEW BODY - NIGHTLY THOUGHTS

Date:

IF I DID NOT WORK OUT TODAY
(FILL OUT THE FOLLOWING)....

How Did I Relax My Body Today?

Today I Allowed Myself:

What Changes Am I Starting To Notice?

Who Tried To Discourage Me From
Working Out Today?

IF I WORKED OUT TODAY
(FILL OUT THE FOLLOWING)....

Work Out Time:

Equipment That I Used Today:

Length Of Time Spent Working Out:

While Working Out Today, I Listened To:

My Exercise Heart Rate:

Did I Have A Workout Partner/Trainer Today
And If The Answer Is Yes, Who Was It?

My Heart Rate Resting:

I Motivated Myself By:

Today I Ate:

My Workout Today Consisted Of:

Today I Drank:

NIGHTLY THOUGHTS CONTINUED

Classes I Took Today (Answer If Applicable):

I Noticed:

What Parts Of My Body Feel Sore Today?

I No Longer Complain About:

What Felt Good Today?

What Tried To Discourage Me Today From Working Out?

What Did Not Feel Good Today?

I Took Advantage Of:

What Was A Challenge For Me Today?

I Am Progressing Towards:

I Am Working Through:

NEW BODY THIS MORNING

Date: Mood:

Today's Declaration:

My Body Is:

My Body Feels:

I Thank God For:

Today I Will Focus On:

My Exercise Goal For Today:

Today's Self-Talk:

390

MY NEW BODY - NIGHTLY THOUGHTS

Date:

IF I DID NOT WORK OUT TODAY
(FILL OUT THE FOLLOWING)....

How Did I Relax My Body Today?

Today I Allowed Myself:

What Changes Am I Starting To Notice?

Who Tried To Discourage Me From Working Out Today?

IF I WORKED OUT TODAY
(FILL OUT THE FOLLOWING)....

Work Out Time:

Equipment That I Used Today:

Length Of Time Spent Working Out:

While Working Out Today, I Listened To:

My Exercise Heart Rate:

Did I Have A Workout Partner/Trainer Today And If The Answer Is Yes, Who Was It?

My Heart Rate Resting:

I Motivated Myself By:

Today I Ate:

My Workout Today Consisted Of:

Today I Drank:

NIGHTLY THOUGHTS CONTINUED

Classes I Took Today (Answer If Applicable):

I Noticed:

What Parts Of My Body Feel Sore Today?

I No Longer Complain About:

What Felt Good Today?

What Tried To Discourage Me Today From Working Out?

What Did Not Feel Good Today?

I Took Advantage Of:

What Was A Challenge For Me Today?

I Am Progressing Towards:

I Am Working Through:

I AM CLOSER THAN I WAS YESTERDAY.

WHAT HAS SURPRISED ME?

NEW BODY THIS MORNING

Date: Mood:

Today's Declaration:

My Body Is:

My Body Feels:

I Thank God For:

Today I Will Focus On:

My Exercise Goal For Today:

Today's Self-Talk:

MY NEW BODY - NIGHTLY THOUGHTS

Date:

IF I DID NOT WORK OUT TODAY
(FILL OUT THE FOLLOWING)....

How Did I Relax My Body Today?

Today I Allowed Myself:

What Changes Am I Starting To Notice?

Who Tried To Discourage Me From
Working Out Today?

IF I WORKED OUT TODAY
(FILL OUT THE FOLLOWING)....

Work Out Time:

Equipment That I Used Today:

Length Of Time Spent Working Out:

While Working Out Today, I Listened To:

My Exercise Heart Rate:

Did I Have A Workout Partner/Trainer Today
And If The Answer Is Yes, Who Was It?

My Heart Rate Resting:

I Motivated Myself By:

Today I Ate:

My Workout Today Consisted Of:

Today I Drank:

NIGHTLY THOUGHTS CONTINUED

Classes I Took Today (Answer If Applicable):

I Noticed:

What Parts Of My Body Feel Sore Today?

I No Longer Complain About:

What Felt Good Today?

What Tried To Discourage Me Today From Working Out?

What Did Not Feel Good Today?

I Took Advantage Of:

What Was A Challenge For Me Today?

I Am Progressing Towards:

I Am Working Through:

NEW BODY THIS MORNING

Date: Mood:

Today's Declaration:

My Body Is:

My Body Feels:

I Thank God For:

Today I Will Focus On:

My Exercise Goal For Today:

Today's Self-Talk:

398

MY NEW BODY – NIGHTLY THOUGHTS

Date:

IF I DID NOT WORK OUT TODAY
(FILL OUT THE FOLLOWING)....

How Did I Relax My Body Today?

Today I Allowed Myself:

What Changes Am I Starting To Notice?

Who Tried To Discourage Me From
Working Out Today?

IF I WORKED OUT TODAY
(FILL OUT THE FOLLOWING)....

Work Out Time:

Equipment That I Used Today:

Length Of Time Spent Working Out:

While Working Out Today, I Listened To:

My Exercise Heart Rate:

Did I Have A Workout Partner/Trainer Today
And If The Answer Is Yes, Who Was It?

My Heart Rate Resting:

I Motivated Myself By:

Today I Ate:

My Workout Today Consisted Of:

Today I Drank:

NIGHTLY THOUGHTS CONTINUED

Classes I Took Today (Answer If Applicable):

I Noticed:

What Parts Of My Body Feel Sore Today?

I No Longer Complain About:

What Felt Good Today?

What Tried To Discourage Me Today From Working Out?

What Did Not Feel Good Today?

I Took Advantage Of:

What Was A Challenge For Me Today?

I Am Progressing Towards:

I Am Working Through:

NEW BODY THIS MORNING

Date: Mood:

Today's Declaration:

My Body Is:

My Body Feels:

I Thank God For:

Today I Will Focus On:

My Exercise Goal For Today:

Today's Self-Talk:

MY NEW BODY - NIGHTLY THOUGHTS

Date:

IF I DID NOT WORK OUT TODAY
(FILL OUT THE FOLLOWING)....

How Did I Relax My Body Today?

Today I Allowed Myself:

What Changes Am I Starting To Notice?

Who Tried To Discourage Me From Working Out Today?

IF I WORKED OUT TODAY
(FILL OUT THE FOLLOWING)....

Work Out Time:

Equipment That I Used Today:

Length Of Time Spent Working Out:

While Working Out Today, I Listened To:

My Exercise Heart Rate:

Did I Have A Workout Partner/Trainer Today And If The Answer Is Yes, Who Was It?

My Heart Rate Resting:

I Motivated Myself By:

Today I Ate:

My Workout Today Consisted Of:

Today I Drank:

Classes I Took Today (Answer If Applicable):

I Noticed:

What Parts Of My Body Feel Sore Today?

I No Longer Complain About:

What Felt Good Today?

What Tried To Discourage Me Today From Working Out?

What Did Not Feel Good Today?

I Took Advantage Of:

What Was A Challenge For Me Today?

I Am Progressing Towards:

I Am Working Through:

CHOOSE TO WORK FOR IT.

IT IS STARTING TO FEEL GOOD.

NEW BODY THIS MORNING

Date: Mood:

Today's Declaration:

My Body Is:

My Body Feels:

I Thank God For:

Today I Will Focus On:

My Exercise Goal For Today:

Today's Self-Talk:

MY NEW BODY - NIGHTLY THOUGHTS

Date:

IF I DID NOT WORK OUT TODAY
(FILL OUT THE FOLLOWING)....

How Did I Relax My Body Today?

Today I Allowed Myself:

What Changes Am I Starting To Notice?

Who Tried To Discourage Me From
Working Out Today?

IF I WORKED OUT TODAY
(FILL OUT THE FOLLOWING)....

Work Out Time:

Equipment That I Used Today:

Length Of Time Spent Working Out:

While Working Out Today, I Listened To:

My Exercise Heart Rate:

Did I Have A Workout Partner/Trainer Today
And If The Answer Is Yes, Who Was It?

My Heart Rate Resting:

I Motivated Myself By:

Today I Ate:

My Workout Today Consisted Of:

Today I Drank:

NIGHTLY THOUGHTS CONTINUED

Classes I Took Today (Answer If Applicable):

I Noticed:

What Parts Of My Body Feel Sore Today?

I No Longer Complain About:

What Felt Good Today?

What Tried To Discourage Me Today From Working Out?

What Did Not Feel Good Today?

I Took Advantage Of:

What Was A Challenge For Me Today?

I Am Progressing Towards:

I Am Working Through:

NEW BODY THIS MORNING

Date: Mood:

Today's Declaration:

My Body Is:

My Body Feels:

I Thank God For:

Today I Will Focus On:

My Exercise Goal For Today:

Today's Self-Talk:

MY NEW BODY - NIGHTLY THOUGHTS

Date:

IF I DID NOT WORK OUT TODAY
(FILL OUT THE FOLLOWING)....

How Did I Relax My Body Today?

Today I Allowed Myself:

What Changes Am I Starting To Notice?

Who Tried To Discourage Me From Working Out Today?

IF I WORKED OUT TODAY
(FILL OUT THE FOLLOWING)....

Work Out Time:

Equipment That I Used Today:

Length Of Time Spent Working Out:

While Working Out Today, I Listened To:

My Exercise Heart Rate:

Did I Have A Workout Partner/Trainer Today And If The Answer Is Yes, Who Was It?

My Heart Rate Resting:

I Motivated Myself By:

Today I Ate:

My Workout Today Consisted Of:

Today I Drank:

NIGHTLY THOUGHTS CONTINUED

Classes I Took Today (Answer If Applicable):

I Noticed:

What Parts Of My Body Feel Sore Today?

I No Longer Complain About:

What Felt Good Today?

What Tried To Discourage Me Today From Working Out?

What Did Not Feel Good Today?

I Took Advantage Of:

What Was A Challenge For Me Today?

I Am Progressing Towards:

I Am Working Through:

EVEN WHEN I FEEL LIKE I CAN NO LONGER DO IT, I FIND THE STRENGTH AND PUSH THROUGH.

PERSONAL THOUGHTS

NEW BODY THIS MORNING

Date: Mood:

Today's Declaration:

My Body Is:

My Body Feels:

I Thank God For:

Today I Will Focus On:

My Exercise Goal For Today:

Today's Self-Talk:

MY NEW BODY - NIGHTLY THOUGHTS

Date:

IF I DID NOT WORK OUT TODAY
(FILL OUT THE FOLLOWING)....

How Did I Relax My Body Today?

Today I Allowed Myself:

What Changes Am I Starting To Notice?

Who Tried To Discourage Me From Working Out Today?

IF I WORKED OUT TODAY
(FILL OUT THE FOLLOWING)....

Work Out Time:

Equipment That I Used Today:

Length Of Time Spent Working Out:

While Working Out Today, I Listened To:

My Exercise Heart Rate:

Did I Have A Workout Partner/Trainer Today And If The Answer Is Yes, Who Was It?

My Heart Rate Resting:

I Motivated Myself By:

Today I Ate:

My Workout Today Consisted Of:

Today I Drank:

NIGHTLY THOUGHTS CONTINUED

Classes I Took Today (Answer If Applicable):

I Noticed:

What Parts Of My Body Feel Sore Today?

I No Longer Complain About:

What Felt Good Today?

What Tried To Discourage Me Today From Working Out?

What Did Not Feel Good Today?

I Took Advantage Of:

What Was A Challenge For Me Today?

I Am Progressing Towards:

I Am Working Through:

NEW BODY THIS MORNING

Date: Mood:

Today's Declaration:

My Body Is:

My Body Feels:

I Thank God For:

Today I Will Focus On:

My Exercise Goal For Today:

Today's Self-Talk:

MY NEW BODY - NIGHTLY THOUGHTS

Date:

IF I DID NOT WORK OUT TODAY
(FILL OUT THE FOLLOWING)....

How Did I Relax My Body Today?

Today I Allowed Myself:

What Changes Am I Starting To Notice?

Who Tried To Discourage Me From Working Out Today?

IF I WORKED OUT TODAY
(FILL OUT THE FOLLOWING)....

Work Out Time:

Equipment That I Used Today:

Length Of Time Spent Working Out:

While Working Out Today, I Listened To:

My Exercise Heart Rate:

Did I Have A Workout Partner/Trainer Today And If The Answer Is Yes, Who Was It?

My Heart Rate Resting:

I Motivated Myself By:

Today I Ate:

My Workout Today Consisted Of:

Today I Drank:

NIGHTLY THOUGHTS CONTINUED

Classes I Took Today (Answer If Applicable):

I Noticed:

What Parts Of My Body Feel Sore Today?

I No Longer Complain About:

What Felt Good Today?

What Tried To Discourage Me Today From Working Out?

What Did Not Feel Good Today?

I Took Advantage Of:

What Was A Challenge For Me Today?

I Am Progressing Towards:

I Am Working Through:

UNLOCKING MY POTENTIAL FEELS GOOD.

I AM OVERCOMING MY FEARS AND GETTING CLOSER TO MY DREAMS.

NEW BODY THIS MORNING

Date: Mood:

Today's Declaration:

My Body Is:

My Body Feels:

I Thank God For:

Today I Will Focus On:

My Exercise Goal For Today:

Today's Self-Talk:

MY NEW BODY - NIGHTLY THOUGHTS

Date:

IF I DID NOT WORK OUT TODAY
(FILL OUT THE FOLLOWING)....

How Did I Relax My Body Today?

Today I Allowed Myself:

What Changes Am I Starting To Notice?

Who Tried To Discourage Me From Working Out Today?

IF I WORKED OUT TODAY
(FILL OUT THE FOLLOWING)....

Work Out Time:

Equipment That I Used Today:

Length Of Time Spent Working Out:

While Working Out Today, I Listened To:

My Exercise Heart Rate:

Did I Have A Workout Partner/Trainer Today And If The Answer Is Yes, Who Was It?

My Heart Rate Resting:

I Motivated Myself By:

Today I Ate:

My Workout Today Consisted Of:

Today I Drank:

NIGHTLY THOUGHTS CONTINUED

Classes I Took Today (Answer If Applicable):

I Noticed:

What Parts Of My Body Feel Sore Today?

I No Longer Complain About:

What Felt Good Today?

What Tried To Discourage Me Today From Working Out?

What Did Not Feel Good Today?

I Took Advantage Of:

What Was A Challenge For Me Today?

I Am Progressing Towards:

I Am Working Through:

NEW BODY THIS MORNING

Date: Mood:

Today's Declaration:

My Body Is:

My Body Feels:

I Thank God For:

Today I Will Focus On:

My Exercise Goal For Today:

Today's Self-Talk:

MY NEW BODY - NIGHTLY THOUGHTS

Date:

IF I DID NOT WORK OUT TODAY
(FILL OUT THE FOLLOWING)....

How Did I Relax My Body Today?

Today I Allowed Myself:

What Changes Am I Starting To Notice?

Who Tried To Discourage Me From Working Out Today?

IF I WORKED OUT TODAY
(FILL OUT THE FOLLOWING)....

Work Out Time:

Equipment That I Used Today:

Length Of Time Spent Working Out:

While Working Out Today, I Listened To:

My Exercise Heart Rate:

Did I Have A Workout Partner/Trainer Today And If The Answer Is Yes, Who Was It?

My Heart Rate Resting:

I Motivated Myself By:

Today I Ate:

My Workout Today Consisted Of:

Today I Drank:

NIGHTLY THOUGHTS CONTINUED

Classes I Took Today (Answer If Applicable):

I Noticed:

What Parts Of My Body Feel Sore Today?

I No Longer Complain About:

What Felt Good Today?

What Tried To Discourage Me Today From Working Out?

What Did Not Feel Good Today?

I Took Advantage Of:

What Was A Challenge For Me Today?

I Am Progressing Towards:

I Am Working Through:

I AM BECOMING....

I AM PUTTING IN THAT WORK!

NEW BODY THIS MORNING

Date: Mood:

Today's Declaration:

My Body Is:

My Body Feels:

I Thank God For:

Today I Will Focus On:

My Exercise Goal For Today:

Today's Self-Talk:

430

MY NEW BODY - NIGHTLY THOUGHTS

Date:

IF I DID NOT WORK OUT TODAY
(FILL OUT THE FOLLOWING)....

How Did I Relax My Body Today?

Today I Allowed Myself:

What Changes Am I Starting To Notice?

Who Tried To Discourage Me From Working Out Today?

IF I WORKED OUT TODAY
(FILL OUT THE FOLLOWING)....

Work Out Time:

Equipment That I Used Today:

Length Of Time Spent Working Out:

While Working Out Today, I Listened To:

My Exercise Heart Rate:

Did I Have A Workout Partner/Trainer Today And If The Answer Is Yes, Who Was It?

My Heart Rate Resting:

I Motivated Myself By:

Today I Ate:

My Workout Today Consisted Of:

Today I Drank:

NIGHTLY THOUGHTS CONTINUED

Classes I Took Today (Answer If Applicable):

I Noticed:

What Parts Of My Body Feel Sore Today?

I No Longer Complain About:

What Felt Good Today?

What Tried To Discourage Me Today From Working Out?

What Did Not Feel Good Today?

I Took Advantage Of:

What Was A Challenge For Me Today?

I Am Progressing Towards:

I Am Working Through:

NEW BODY THIS MORNING

Date: Mood:

Today's Declaration:

My Body Is:

My Body Feels:

I Thank God For:

Today I Will Focus On:

My Exercise Goal For Today:

Today's Self-Talk:

MY NEW BODY - NIGHTLY THOUGHTS

Date:

IF I DID NOT WORK OUT TODAY
(FILL OUT THE FOLLOWING)....

How Did I Relax My Body Today?

Today I Allowed Myself:

What Changes Am I Starting To Notice?

Who Tried To Discourage Me From Working Out Today?

IF I WORKED OUT TODAY
(FILL OUT THE FOLLOWING)....

Work Out Time:

Equipment That I Used Today:

Length Of Time Spent Working Out:

While Working Out Today, I Listened To:

My Exercise Heart Rate:

Did I Have A Workout Partner/Trainer Today And If The Answer Is Yes, Who Was It?

My Heart Rate Resting:

I Motivated Myself By:

Today I Ate:

My Workout Today Consisted Of:

Today I Drank:

NIGHTLY THOUGHTS CONTINUED

Classes I Took Today (Answer If Applicable):

I Noticed:

What Parts Of My Body Feel Sore Today?

I No Longer Complain About:

What Felt Good Today?

What Tried To Discourage Me Today From Working Out?

What Did Not Feel Good Today?

I Took Advantage Of:

What Was A Challenge For Me Today?

I Am Progressing Towards:

I Am Working Through:

NEW BODY THIS MORNING

Date: Mood:

Today's Declaration:

My Body Is:

My Body Feels:

I Thank God For:

Today I Will Focus On:

My Exercise Goal For Today:

Today's Self-Talk:

MY NEW BODY – NIGHTLY THOUGHTS

Date:

IF I DID NOT WORK OUT TODAY
(FILL OUT THE FOLLOWING)....

How Did I Relax My Body Today?

What Changes Am I Starting To Notice?

Today I Allowed Myself:

Who Tried To Discourage Me From
Working Out Today?

IF I WORKED OUT TODAY
(FILL OUT THE FOLLOWING)....

Work Out Time:

Length Of Time Spent Working Out:

My Exercise Heart Rate:

My Heart Rate Resting:

I Motivated Myself By:

My Workout Today Consisted Of:

Equipment That I Used Today:

While Working Out Today, I Listened To:

Did I Have A Workout Partner/Trainer Today
And If The Answer Is Yes, Who Was It?

Today I Ate:

Today I Drank:

Classes I Took Today (Answer If Applicable):

What Parts Of My Body Feel Sore Today?

What Felt Good Today?

What Did Not Feel Good Today?

What Was A Challenge For Me Today?

I Am Working Through:

I Noticed:

I No Longer Complain About:

What Tried To Discourage Me Today From Working Out?

I Took Advantage Of:

I Am Progressing Towards:

WHEN I STAY FOCUS, I....

WHAT IS HOLDING ME BACK FROM BEING MY BEST SELF?

NEW BODY THIS MORNING

Date: Mood:

Today's Declaration:

My Body Is:

My Body Feels:

I Thank God For:

Today I Will Focus On:

My Exercise Goal For Today:

Today's Self-Talk:

MY NEW BODY - NIGHTLY THOUGHTS

Date:

IF I DID NOT WORK OUT TODAY
(FILL OUT THE FOLLOWING)....

How Did I Relax My Body Today?

Today I Allowed Myself:

What Changes Am I Starting To Notice?

Who Tried To Discourage Me From Working Out Today?

IF I WORKED OUT TODAY
(FILL OUT THE FOLLOWING)....

Work Out Time:

Equipment That I Used Today:

Length Of Time Spent Working Out:

While Working Out Today, I Listened To:

My Exercise Heart Rate:

Did I Have A Workout Partner/Trainer Today And If The Answer Is Yes, Who Was It?

My Heart Rate Resting:

I Motivated Myself By:

Today I Ate:

My Workout Today Consisted Of:

Today I Drank:

NIGHTLY THOUGHTS CONTINUED

Classes I Took Today (Answer If Applicable):

I Noticed:

What Parts Of My Body Feel Sore Today?

I No Longer Complain About:

What Felt Good Today?

What Tried To Discourage Me Today From Working Out?

What Did Not Feel Good Today?

I Took Advantage Of:

What Was A Challenge For Me Today?

I Am Progressing Towards:

I Am Working Through:

NEW BODY THIS MORNING

Date: Mood:

Today's Declaration:

My Body Is:

My Body Feels:

I Thank God For:

Today I Will Focus On:

My Exercise Goal For Today:

Today's Self-Talk:

MY NEW BODY - NIGHTLY THOUGHTS

Date:

IF I DID NOT WORK OUT TODAY
(FILL OUT THE FOLLOWING)....

How Did I Relax My Body Today?

Today I Allowed Myself:

What Changes Am I Starting To Notice?

Who Tried To Discourage Me From Working Out Today?

IF I WORKED OUT TODAY
(FILL OUT THE FOLLOWING)....

Work Out Time:

Equipment That I Used Today:

Length Of Time Spent Working Out:

While Working Out Today, I Listened To:

My Exercise Heart Rate:

Did I Have A Workout Partner/Trainer Today And If The Answer Is Yes, Who Was It?

My Heart Rate Resting:

I Motivated Myself By:

Today I Ate:

My Workout Today Consisted Of:

Today I Drank:

NIGHTLY THOUGHTS CONTINUED

Classes I Took Today (Answer If Applicable):

I Noticed:

What Parts Of My Body Feel Sore Today?

I No Longer Complain About:

What Felt Good Today?

What Tried To Discourage Me Today From Working Out?

What Did Not Feel Good Today?

I Took Advantage Of:

What Was A Challenge For Me Today?

I Am Progressing Towards:

I Am Working Through:

ALL THAT WORK IS PAYING OFF.

Made in the USA
Columbia, SC
23 September 2023

23204197R00243